PROPERTY INSPECTION:
AN APPRAISER'S GUIDE

JOHN A. SIMPSON, MAI

Readers of this text may be interested in these related text published by the Appraisal Institute:

The Appraisal of Real Estate, eleventh edition
Appraising Residential Properties, second edition
Environmental Site Assessments and Their Impact on Property Value: The Appraiser's Role
Shopping Center Appraisal and Analysis
Subdivision Analysis

For a catalog of Appraisal Institute publications, contact the PR/Marketing Department of the Appraisal Institute, 875 N. Michigan Ave., Suite 2400, Chicago, IL 60611-1980

Property Inspection: An Appraiser's Guide

JOHN A. SIMPSON, MAI

APPRAISAL
INSTITUTE®

875 N. Michigan Avenue
Chicago, Illinois 60611-1980

Reviewers:
Frank E. Harrison, MAI, SRA
Thomas A. Motta, MAI, SRA
Janice F. Young, MAI, RM

Senior Vice President, Communications: Christopher Bettin
Manager, Book Development: Michael R. Milgrim, PhD
Senior Editor/Writer: Stephanie Shea-Joyce
Manager, Design/Production: Julie B. Beich
Graphic Designer: Claire Baldwin

For Educational Purposes Only

The material presented in this text has been reviewed by members of the Appraisal Institute, but the opinions and procedures set forth by the author are not necessarily endorsed as the only methodology consistent with proper appraisal practice. While a great deal of care has been taken to provide accurate and current information, neither the Appraisal Institute nor its editors and staff assume responsibility for the accuracy of the data contained herein. Further, the general principles and conclusions presented in this text are subject to local, state, and federal laws and regulations, court cases, and any revisions of the same. This publication is sold for educational purposes with the understanding that the publisher is not engaged in rendering legal, accounting, or other professional service.

Nondiscrimination Policy

Printed in the United States of America

01 00 99 98 97   5 4 3 2 1

Library of Congress Cataloging-in-Publication Data

Simpson, John A. (John Andrew), 1962-
    Property inspection / John A. Simpson.
          p.   cm.
    Includes bibliographical references.
    ISBN 0-922154-36-8
    1. Building inspection.   2. Buildings—Valuation.   3. Real property—Valuation.   I. Title.
TH439.S54   1997
        333.33'2'0285—dc21

                                                    97-3831
                                                      CIP

TABLE OF CONTENTS

FOREWORD

Property inspection is probably the most visible, hands-on part of an appraiser's job. Most property owners see the need for this task and have a general understanding of its place in the appraisal process. Although property inspection is a vital part of any appraisal of real property, there is a surprisingly amount of diversity in how appraisers undertake inspections.

Because few appraisal firms provide formal training and guidelines for the inspection of property, many appraisers teach themselves, basing their observations on common sense and experience. Eventually, most practitioners get a sense of what to look for in a property and how the market will perceive what they see. Unfortunately, this process has a long learning curve and provides mixed results.

This new text, *Property Inspection: An Appraiser's Guide,* provides a systematic overview of the inspection of homes, commercial properties, and the sites on which they are built. It explores the inspection tools available to appraisers today and demonstrates the importance of preparation, thoroughness, and data verification. Careful attention is paid to the appraiser's responsibility to identify property defects, assess potential hazards, and verify data sources. The business risk inherent in the inspection process is examined and useful tips for limiting liability and improving competence are provided. A clear distinction is made between the knowledge expected of appraisers and the expertise demanded of engineers, surveyors, home inspectors, and other professionals involved in property inspections.

The Appraisal Institute is proud to present this text, which provides practical techniques and advice that will make appraisers more comfortable with property inspections and more competent in their execution.

Kenneth L. Nicholson, SRA
1997 President
Appraisal Institute

ABOUT THE AUTHOR

John Simpson, MAI, is a partner in Total Real Estate Services, a residential and commercial real estate appraisal and brokerage firm in Crofton, Maryland. Simpson has appraised a wide range of commercial properties throughout New Jersey and Pennsylvania. He has contributed to current appraisal theory on recycling stations and cooperative apartment leasehold valuations and has had a number of his articles published in *The Appraisal Journal* and other real estate publications. Simpson has received bachelor's degrees in business administration and management from Rutgers University as well as a master's of business administration degree in real estate and management from Temple University. He can be reached via e-mail at appraiser@erols.com.

PREFACE

Property inspection is a skill an appraiser often learns by doing and by example. Formal property inspection training programs for appraisers are few. With increased competition and greater emphasis on quality to maintain a customer base, appraisers are finding that property inspection is more important than ever. One crucial mistake made during a property inspection can lead to embarrassment, loss of a client, or even a lawsuit. State regulation has added to the appraiser's responsibility. Appraisers who are licensed or certified are now accountable to the state in addition to any professional organization to which they may belong. Thus, inexperienced appraisers need to develop property inspection skills to limit business risk.

This book has been written to help appraisers, whose property inspection training, knowledge, and experience vary widely. It provides a standardized body of property inspection knowledge, which can be used as a training tool for novice appraisers and as a review for more experienced practitioners. The text focuses on aspects of property inspection for which an appraiser is responsible and on methods for reducing business risk through appropriate property inspection techniques. This book has *not* been designed to make an appraiser a home or commercial building inspector. Technical aspects of building construction, engineering, and environmental site analysis are not covered. Appraisers are not expected to be experts in such areas and are not accountable for expertise beyond what a typical appraiser should know.

To increase its usefulness, this book offers two types of "tips." Text boxes identified as "Appraiser's Tips" relate to items that the appraiser has significant liability to report within an appraisal. Boxes labeled "Inspector's Tips" provide additional information that may be helpful to the appraiser, but for which he or she is not likely to be held accountable.

A secondary goal of this book is to help appraisal offices develop efficient property inspection programs. A large part of an appraiser's job is collecting and analyzing data. Without adequate property inspection techniques, subject and comparable analyses cannot be performed accurately. Poor inspection techniques can result in faulty assumptions, incorrect values, and added business risk. Unfortunately, many appraisers do not realize how great a risk they take in the area of property inspection. The author hopes that this text will point out some of these risks and provide a learning tool for entry-level appraisers, a reference for experienced appraisers, and a valuable business resource for owners and managers of appraisal firms.

ACKNOWLEDGMENTS

Many people helped make this book possible. I would like to thank Eleanor Gunn, MAI, Robert D. Clifford, MAI, RM, and Everett Moore, MAI for their insights and ideas. No dedication would be complete without special thanks to my mother, Edna Simpson, about whom I could never say enough. Eileen Chmielewski, my partner, was invaluable and I am very grateful for her support. I would also like to thank Greg and Judy Moy for their eternal friendship.

CHAPTER 1

THE IMPORTANCE OF PROPERTY INSPECTION

ince appraisal is a service industry, the competitive position of an appraiser or an appraisal firm is at least partially tied to property inspection abilities. Learning inspection skills and properly applying them are critical to becoming a successful appraiser.

Property inspection provides the foundation for the analyses that comprise an appraisal. The identification of important physical features of a subject property and comparable properties and the validation of these data are critical to value analyses and opinions.

Two problems inherent in occupations based on technical expertise are the length of time it takes one to become proficient and the amount of continuing education required to remain so. The old adage, "There's no substitute for experience," is especially applicable to technical fields and the appraisal profession is no exception. Appraisers often learn property inspection on their own. The result is a wide variation in inspection skills, depending on what types of properties have been appraised, what types of learning situations arose from the appraisals, and, if the appraiser is affiliated with a large firm, how much support was provided by the firm. For these reasons it takes many years for appraisers to become proficient in this area and they constantly find new things to learn.

The importance of property inspection cannot be overemphasized. According to data compiled by Liability Insurance Administrators, failure to disclose property defects is one of the major reasons for errors and omissions claims against appraisers (see Table 1.1)[1]. As cited in the table, 11% of all claims against appraisers in 1994 resulted from failure to disclose defects in a property. Such failures probably relate to poor inspection practices or knowledge.

These claims typically arise after the buyers discover such defects as termite infestation, cracked foundations, structural damage, or settling. An appraiser who doesn't note these conditions in the appraisal report may be deemed negligent by

---

1. Robert Wiley, "Liability Insurance Corner," *Appraiser Gram* (December 1994), 3.

the buyers. Although there is conflicting case history as to an appraiser's duty to disclose such defects, you shouldn't take the chance that you won't be held responsible. It is important to note any condition you observe during the course of a physical inspection. The use of disclaimers to limiting conditions in your report can also limit your exposure.[2]

Failure to verify information concerning square footage, zoning, sewer/septic tank hookup, water, floodplains, and a wide range of other items also undermine the property inspection process. Such failures have resulted in 28% of reported E&O claims and can lead to inaccurate valuations. Obviously, property inspection skills and knowledge are a key component in minimizing business risk, maintaining competitive position, and avoiding lawsuits.

Table 1.1—Claims Against Appraisers for 1994	
REASON FOR CLAIM	PERCENTAGE OF CLAIMS
Overappraisal of property	31%
Failure to verify information	28%
Failure to disclose defects in subject	11%
Alleged fraud or deliberate conspiracy on the part of the appraiser	4%
Appraiser-client disputes regarding fees, slander, or breach of duty	7%
Underappraisal of property	7%
Miscellaneous negligence suits	12%

Source: Liability Insurance Administrators

PROPERTY INSPECTION AND THE APPRAISAL PROCESS

Nearly every aspect of the appraisal process is based on property inspection skills. The three traditional valuation methods—the cost approach, sales comparison approach, and income capitalization approach—are based on inspection of the subject and comparable properties. The validity of the sales comparison approach depends directly and critically on the inspection of the subject and comparables sales. The cost approach is based on the physical inspection of the subject site and comparable vacant land sales as well as a comparison of the subject to cost comparables (from a cost service) or actual construction cost comparables. The income

---

2. Ibid.

capitalization approach requires a comparison of the subject and rental comparables. Applicable expenses of the subject are often compared to other expense comparables on a physical basis. Even the overall capitalization rates selected depend on the physical features and competitiveness of the subject.

Other parts of the appraisal report, including descriptions of the site and improvements and the analysis of the subject within its market, are based on inspection skills. The section on zoning considers the physical features of a property, and the tax assessment section details tax data based on the value of the land and the cost of constructing the improvements. Highest and best use analysis—the key to the selection of comparable properties and the entire valuation—hinges on the physical attributes of the site and buildings. Obviously, the appraiser's work—the reason he or she has been hired—relies heavily on property inspection skills, which are paramount to reaching an informed and well-reasoned value conclusion.

PROPERTY INSPECTION AND COURT TESTIMONY

Appraisers who have testified in court can attest to the importance of observing and analyzing details about the subject, the comparables, and the market. These functions have property inspection as their foundation. Having even one comparable sale or rental rejected in court can make the difference between winning and losing a case (or a client).

Appraisers who testify in court rely heavily on the sales comparison approach. For all but the most atypical property types, the sales comparison approach often receives equal or greater weight than the other valuation approaches, for which information such as lease and operating expense data may be difficult to obtain. The degree to which comparable properties are inspected directly affects the validity of an appraiser's analyses and the strength of his or her position. If an appraiser is unable to inspect the interior of a comparable or a property prior to its renovation, the comparison may not be defensible. Given the importance of the sales comparison approach to the final value conclusion, inspection plays a key role in valuations and the results of court cases.

PROPERTY INSPECTION AND FINANCIAL INSTITUTIONS

Appraisers convey their opinions and analyses differently depending on the needs of the client. Appraisals for court often emphasize comparable data and adjustments, while appraisals for banks tend to emphasize physical and market factors that affect the property. Although the numerical analyses may be similar, the presentation of the report is tailored to the client.

Financial institutions are very concerned with the competitiveness of a property. Because loan terms cover many years, items of obsolescence are a major concern to financial institutions. If a property suffers from obsolescence, it may not have a competitive market position over the mortgage term. If the property is repossessed, obsolescence usually results in a prolonged marketing period, additional marketing expenses, and often significant discounts from the original mortgage amount. Property inspection skills and the method used to convey property information are critical to a proper understanding of the collateral for the loan.

PROPERTY INSPECTION IN TODAY'S MARKETS

Since the overwhelming majority of commercial properties are considered noninvestment grade, the sales comparison approach is often at least as important as the income capitalization approach in commercial valuations. For smaller commercial properties, the sales comparison approach is usually considered the primary value indicator. The recent approval by financial institutions of the use of limited scope appraisals for their performing loans or loan renewals results in almost exclusive use of the sales comparison approach. Of course, the sales comparison approach is the primary value indicator in most residential appraisals, and property inspection skills are the key to proper analysis.

Given the increased accountability of the appraisal profession, well-developed inspection skills along with sound numerical analyses are essential in acquiring and maintaining working relationships with banks. The widely publicized savings and loan crisis shed new light on the role of real estate appraisers within the lending process. Financial institutions can select the most qualified appraisers from the large pool of appraisers available.

In addition to their greater accountability, appraisers are often considered the "front line" when potential problems arise. Less than half of the home buyers in this country use home inspectors, so the appraiser is often the only "unbiased" person looking at the property. Appraisers have a duty to point out to the client any potential problems observed. Unfortunately, appraisers spend most of their time taking notes on the construction and condition of a home without probing deeper. Problems with the expensive components of a home or commercial building can kill a deal, and the appraiser may be blamed for not noting problems within the appraisal. No one wants to pay legal fees or go through the hassle of being the first to establish case law limiting an appraiser's liability on a particular component of a property.

CHAPTER 2

DEVELOPING AN INSPECTION SYSTEM

Few appraisers or appraisal firms have formal property inspection systems. It is very common to see experienced appraisers writing their inspection notes on blank pads of paper because no universally accepted inspection form exists. Many firms do not take the time to develop inspection forms, although some larger, more established firms have standardized forms for the subject property, comparable land sales, improved sales, and rentals. Unfortunately, very few firms verify that the forms are being filled out properly, if at all.

PROPERTY INSPECTION FORMS

Without an efficient property inspection system in place, appraisers will not want to use forms designed for their benefit. In turn, inspection and appraisal quality will be highly variable and business risk will be increased. For an efficient property inspection system, the forms used

1. Should request only relevant information. Extraneous information or questions should be removed.
2. Should be formatted to request data in the sequence a typical appraiser inspects a property.
3. Should be flexible so that they can be customized to suit the style of the appraiser.
4. Should be easy to fill out, using checkboxes, multiple-choice questions, and blank lines wherever appropriate.
5. Should include one or more lines for verification.

Finally, the forms must be accepted by the appraisers who will use them. Practitioners should understand the reasoning behind each form and their suggestions for improvement should be elicited. Periodic review of the forms being used also helps ensure consistency and reduce business risk.

RELEVANT INSPECTION INFORMATION

Some items noticed during an inspection are common to all properties, some are applicable only to specific property types, and some are applicable only rarely. For inspection forms to be relevant, they must ask the right questions at the right time.

In a large office, a good starting point for developing relevant forms is to obtain input from as many appraisers as possible. The appraisers can meet to decide on the goals of each form, the questions to be asked, and the form's overall design. Although one person can design the forms, more information and creativity are generated from a group. More important, appraisers who provide input in developing the forms are more likely to understand them and use them in the field.

After laying out all the information to be included in the forms, the items can be further classified for inclusion. If an item is common to all property types, such as the frame of the building or size of the site, it should go on all the forms. If the item is applicable only to certain property types, e.g., loading doors for an industrial building or elevators for an office building, it should be indicated only on forms for that property type.

After selecting the items to be shown on the various forms, each item should be considered for relevance. Is the item common to every appraisal of that property type or is it rarely seen? Is the item important to a client? Does not having it on the form increase business risk? Answering these questions suggests if an item is relevant and worthy of inclusion. If it is important and common, it should go on the form; if not, it is extraneous and should be excluded.

ARRANGING INFORMATION SEQUENTIALLY

Organizing the information according to where data can be found and where it will be discussed within the appraisal report is helpful. Information may be found at municipal offices or departments, at the subject property, or at comparable properties. The easier it is for the appraiser to gather information and organize it for presentation within the report, the easier the inspection process will become.

For instance, questions about the subject site's physical description should be covered in one section. Site information such as the amount of wetlands or the flood zone designation, which may be found at municipal offices, may be grouped under a "Municipal" heading with the subheading "Engineer's Office." This will help the appraiser ask the appropriate officials the right questions with the least amount of time and effort. Good organization can eliminate additional telephone calls or trips to get information that could have been acquired during the initial visit.

CUSTOMIZING FORMS

Appraisers have their own methods of inspection. Some appraisers prefer to go to the municipality first and then to the subject property. Others prefer to reverse the tasks. Some appraisers visit a comparable sale before going to the municipality to verify the information, while others do the opposite. Highly experienced appraisers like condensed forms, while novices may prefer longer forms with more questions. As long as all relevant items are included, forms can be designed to serve the user.

Customizing a form to each appraiser's preferences allows for greater efficiency and increases the likelihood of the form being used. Customization also encourages appraisers to augment the forms over time, thus improving them further.

REMOVING EXTRANEOUS INFORMATION

Some inspection forms are plagued by redundancy and extraneous information. Asking irrelevant questions makes the appraiser appear unorganized and unprofessional. The goal should be to create forms that cover the relevant information with a minimum of paperwork. Reducing the number of questions to be asked allows for an efficient question-and-answer session between the appraiser and the property representative.

CONVENIENCE

If a form is to be used, it must be kept simple. Forms that are not user-friendly will not be completed or will be completed incorrectly. Phrasing questions concisely, providing multiple-choice answers, and directing questions to the proper person at the right time are the keys to well-designed inspection forms.

VERIFICATION

To limit business risk, all forms should have blanks for verification, where the name of the person spoken to, the date of the interview, and perhaps the contact's phone number are provided. Since an appraiser may be called on to testify or answer questions years after an appraisal has been completed, this type of documentation is important. It allows the appraiser to cite the source of the information contained in the report. Having the date of the interview and what the person said on the form can prevent misunderstandings. The appraiser should get in the habit of asking for verification information to reduce business risk.

RATIONALE FOR THE FORM

For a form to be successful, the appraisers must understand the reasoning behind it. In a large office, this can be explained in the first meeting of supervisors and field appraisers before the forms are designed. Getting the cooperation of everyone involved will be easier if they understand why their input is needed. The goals, purpose, and logic underlying each form should be explained and a consensus reached.

PERIODIC REVIEW

Periodic review of inspection forms helps ensure that they are being filled out consistently and properly. If certain patterns of incomplete answers become evident, this may signal a small or large problem. For instance, if the verification section is consistently left blank, the section may be regularly overlooked, in which case the form may need to be redesigned. On the other hand, the appraisers may be ignoring the section because they are not verifying data, which is a more significant issue because verification limits business risk. As another example, appraisers may neglect to fill out the book and page numbers where the mortgage is recorded on comparable sale forms. This may indicate that the appraisers are not looking at the mortgages and are making adjustments based on information they did not gather, another risky practice. Periodic meetings with appraisers in a group or individually may be necessary to correct this deficiency.

SUGGESTIONS FOR FORM CONSTRUCTION

With the characteristics of an efficient property inspection system in mind, a useful form can be constructed. Four types of information are necessary: 1) headings to make the report easier to reference, 2) the questions themselves, 3) a format for recording answers, and 4) blank spaces for more information or atypical answers.

HEADINGS

Grouping questions by category and placing them under headings simplifies referencing and organizes the information for eventual transcription to the appraisal report. When inspection time is limited, headings help the appraiser locate the questions to be asked quickly.

FORMATS FOR QUESTIONS AND ANSWERS

To design a manageable form, the format for the questions should be concise. Full sentences are not necessary; bulleted questions will usually suffice. Question marks help distinguish a question from an observation.

The easiest formats are multiple-choice and open-ended. Multiple-choice questions tend to be close-ended unless a category for "other" is included, with a blank provided to describe what "other" means. Offering check boxes or responses that can be circled allows appraisers to answer multiple-choice questions quickly.

Open-ended questions are common on forms, but they provide less consistency. For instance, if "Type of roof" is followed by a blank line, the appraiser may just fill in "asphalt," when a more thorough answer such as "flat, rolled-on asphalt," "flat tar and gravel," or "pitched gable" would be more descriptive.

The best format is generally a combination of multiple-choice and open-ended questions. The answer choices provided cover the overwhelming majority of responses, and the blanks allow for customized or atypical answers. If appraisers continually fill in the blank lines on a form, however, it may be a sign that the choice of answers given should be revised.

The property inspection form shown in Figure 2.1 incorporates the features discussed in this section. Figure 2.2 is a "to do" checklist that can be used to gather and verify property information.

SUMMARY

To gather data efficiently, an appraisal firm should have a formal property inspection system, which includes the development and use of property inspection forms. Inspection forms should be:

- Relevant
- Sequential
- Flexible
- Concise
- Convenient
- Completed to provide verification for data
- Designed with the input of all appraisers
- Accepted by users

If the guidelines presented in this chapter are followed, the forms created will be a valuable tool for training appraisers. Moreover, using standardized forms will reduce business risk and result in a coordinated data gathering program.

Figure 2.1—General Property Inspection Form

Property type	Block/lot
Address	Inspection date
City State	Zoning

Ownership/Prior Sale Information ⟵ _Sequentially designed based on the source of the information_

Owner's name	Sale book/page
Address	Other
City State Zip	

Assessment and Real Estate Taxes

Land	Tax rate/year
Building	Equalization ratio
Total	Last reval. effective

Site Description

Land size	Storm sewers
Topography	Fire hydrants
Curbing	Parking spaces
Sidewalks	Garages
Street lights	Other

	Yes	No	N/A	Comments		Yes	No	N/A	Comments
Tax map	○	○	○	_____	Tax collector	○	○	○	_____
Zoning copied	○	○	○	_____	Copy of deed	○	○	○	_____
Zoning map	○	○	○	_____	Water available	○	○	○	_____
Flood map	○	○	○	_____	Water moratorium	○	○	○	_____
Approval status	○	○	○	_____	Sewer available	○	○	○	_____
Affordable housing	○	○	○	_____	Sewer moratorium	○	○	○	_____
Rent control	○	○	○	_____	Highway access mgmt. code	○	○	○	_____

Figure 2.1– General Property Inspection Form (continued)

Comments/Additional Information

_____

_____

General Building Information
(Check off or circle)

	Yes	No	Comments
Sprinklered	O	O	_____
Basement	O	O	_____
ADA conformance*	O	O	_____
Year built			_____
Fire alarm	O	O	_____
Hooked into	FD	Monitor service	
Burglar alarm	O	O	_____
Hooked into	PD	Monitor service	
Frame	Wood	Steel	
Roof	Tar	Metal Rubber Other	

*Americans with Disabilities Act

Roof condition   Good   Fair   Poor

Last roof repair   Patched   Resurfaced   When?_____

Roof guarantee   None   25 yr.   20 yr.   15 yr.   Other____

Loading doors:

Tailgate # ____ Levelers___ Manual___ Power ___

Drive-in # ____ Levelers___ Manual___ Power ___

Low height # ____ Levelers___ Manual___ Power ___

Heating   Gas   Oil   Electric heat pump

Elevatored   No   Yes # ____ lbs. capacity ____

                    # persons capacity _____

How many tons is the A/C? _____

Ceiling height _____ Gross _____ Clear

Multiple-choice answers for questions requiring more than a Yes/No answer

General Site Information

	Yes	No	N/A	Comments
Wetlands	O	O	O	_____
HAZMAT	O	O	O	_____
Added approvals	O	O	O	

	Yes	No	N/A	Comments
Underground tanks	O	O	O	_____
Rail access	O	O	O	_____

Faster, user-friendly way to record predetermined answers

Other Questions

Subject listed for sale, contracted or optioned?
      Yes   No   Get copy

Loan amount, interest rate, term, etc.
_____

Building insurance expense per year

_____

Comments/Additional Information

_____

_____

_____

_____

Ample room for comments here and on the back of each page

Figure 2.2—To Do Checklist

○ Deed	○ Calls to brokers
○ Income and expense	○ _____
○ Calls to other appraisers	○ _____
○ Plans copied	○ _____
○ Rent roll	

File Memoranda

← *File memoranda section for verification and history of all contacts made for this job*

DATE	PERSON	PHONE #	RESULT

← *Concise form length; extraneous information removed*

CHAPTER 3

INSPECTION TOOLS

The inspection tools used by appraisers generally fall into three categories: hardware, accessories, and computer tools. Basic tools such as a camera, clipboard, and measuring wheel or tape are used in every assignment. Tools such as a flashlight, magnet, level, and ice pick can come in handy depending on the property and the extent of inspection permitted by the property owner. Computer sketching programs and imaging software are being used more frequently in the inspection process.

HARDWARE

MEASURING TOOLS

Measuring wheel or tape

The most common tool used in inspections is a measuring wheel or measuring tape. A tape provides more exact measurements, but it is sometimes not possible or practical to measure a building using a tape. A measuring wheel is faster and may be the only way to measure a building if the owner is not cooperative. Because typical measuring tapes only measure up to 200 feet, it is usually more

APPRAISER'S TIP

Shrubs, trees, and man-made objects can make it difficult to measure a large commercial building or a home accurately. When confronted with obstacles, many appraisers use a measuring wheel, which can result in less reliable estimates, especially when multiple sides of a building are affected. The solution is to use a hook and stake tool. A small steel stake is placed in the ground and the appraiser hooks a measuring tape to it. An accurate reading can then be obtained. The hook and stake tool costs about $5 and should be part of every appraiser's tool kit. Figure 3.1 shows a hook and stake tool and illustrates its use.

convenient to use a wheel to measure a large building. Measuring tapes are used by both residential and commercial appraisers, while measuring wheels are commonly used by commercial appraisers.

Ultrasonic measuring devices

Ultrasonic electronic devices are frequently used by residential appraisers to obtain interior room measurements, but they are rarely employed by commercial appraisers. The handheld device, which is about the size of a calculator, is pointed toward a wall and emits a series of sound waves. The distance to the wall is determined by the amount of time it takes for the sound waves to return to the device. These instruments are very accurate, but have a limited range, usually 30 feet or less. Most appraisers prefer ultrasonic measuring devices that are silent and do not emit beeps or other distracting sounds. These devices can be excellent for determining the clear span in industrial buildings or assessing ceiling height when no other means of measurement is available.

Miscellaneous measuring equipment

In addition to measuring wheels, tapes, and ultrasonic devices, the appraiser may find an engineering ruler or architect's scale useful, especially if the only way to measure a building is from preliminary plans. A folding ruler, protractor, or angle iron can also come in handy for measuring corners and angles. These tools can be a great help in determining the size of irregular-shaped areas.

OTHER TOOLS

The well-equipped appraiser will have the following items on hand during an inspection:

- An ice pick, screwdriver, or pocket knife to check wooden beams for termites and to remove the cover of an electrical outlet to determine the type and extent of wall insulation.

- A level to determine the direction of water runoff in the event of a leak. A level can also be used on a flat roof to determine where water will pool and may cause leakage. Some appraisers use a marble to check if floors are level.

- A compass to help determine the orientation of a property, especially on hilly terrain.

- Extra camera batteries in case of battery failure.

- A voltage detector to determine if appliances are properly grounded, if a risk of electrical fire exists, or if an electrical panel is "hot." (A hot panel could severely injure or even kill a person who touches it.)

- A flashlight for inspecting attics and other poorly lighted areas.

- A magnet to determine if plumbing pipes are made of iron.

Dictation Equipment

Dictation devices allow the appraiser to record an item-by-item account of his or her observations as the inspection progresses. Appraisers who frequently testify in court use such devices because it is easier to maintain a mental image of the items observed when there is a sequential record of the inspection. Written notes can be difficult to decipher and, if the appraiser is rushed through the inspection, more can be recorded on tape than can be written down. Although dictated notes require transcription at the office, usually more detail can be derived with this method.

Accessories

The following accessories can also come in handy:

- Clipboards, which are standard equipment in the appraisal industry. Many appraisers prefer metal clipboards with room to store paperwork and forms underneath. Some clipboards also have a plastic cover over the pad so that if it rains, the ink will not be smeared. More elaborate clipboards even have built-in calculators.

- Special pens with ink that does not freeze. Many appraisers simply use a pencil when the temperature drops below freezing.

- A financial calculator (e.g., Hewlett Packard HP-12C or Texas Instruments Business Analyst II).

- A briefcase for carrying inspection forms, measuring equipment, calculators, etc.

- Graph paper for outlining a building's dimensions.

- Waterproof boots or galoshes for rainy days or muddy sites, especially those without paving.

- One or more jackets and a change of clothes. The appraiser should dress comfortably when inspecting roofs and attics; neglecting these areas increases business risk. An appraiser who fails to examine a flat commercial roof or go into the attic of a home for fear of soiling his or her clothes may be accused of negligence.

- Binoculars to examine a gable roof or the upper stories of a commercial property.

APPRAISER'S TIP

Since it is not uncommon for an appraiser to be questioned by neighbors and even the police in the course of a property inspection, it is wise to carry identification. A wallet-size copy of your state appraiser's license, a business card, or appraisal forms may serve to validate your business intentions.

COMPUTER SOFTWARE AND HARDWARE

Appraisers increasingly use computer software to sketch a building's dimensions and create photographic images.

SKETCHING SOFTWARE

Sketching software, which is used more frequently by residential appraisers than commercial appraisers, has progressed to the point where it can provide almost everything an appraiser needs, from home furniture and fixture icons to automatic square footage calculations and area closures. Nevertheless, the appraisal industry has been slow to adopt such software because its interfaces are still somewhat complicated and reminiscent of computer-aided design screens. Appraisers need software with a simple interface that has a short learning curve so that an appraiser who does not use the program for a while can come back to it with little or no difficulty. It should also have some type of mouse or pen drawing capability and a high degree of intelligence to interpret when to flatten lines and draw curves. The ability to plot square footages based on input dimensions and direction is another asset.

IMAGING

Software

Imaging programs capture photographic images from specialized cameras or camcorders and download the pictures to a computer program. This allows the image to be printed and used repeatedly.

The primary users of digital imaging are residential appraisers. The volume of photographic images required in a residential appraisal report is such that film processing costs are very high in comparison to the appraisal fee. The transition to digital imaging has been rapid due to Fannie Mae's desire for electronic transmission of residential appraisals. Imaging systems are increasingly necessary because the only other way to prepare images for transmission involves considerable cost—i.e., to develop the film, have the images scanned, and then manipulate the images with scanning software. Obviously, this process is more time-consuming and expensive than using image camera downloading.

Imaging software falls into two categories: 1) software to interface between the computer hardware and the camera, and 2) compression utilities. When imaging was in its infancy, the image from the camera had to be downloaded to an image capture utility and then translated into the software used to prepare the appraisal report. Fortunately, this capture utility has been incorporated into many appraisal software programs and, when external capture software must be used, it is often "invisible" as it works with the appraisal software.

Compression utilities are extremely important in determining if imaging software is practical. Saving a picture in color requires a significant amount of disk storage, depending on the format used to save the photograph and the balance of resolution and color depth desired by the user. Using a typical resolution setting, 40 to 50 pictures can be stored in one megabyte of hard disk space, generally enough for about six residential appraisal reports. Compression software is now being included in the interface and/or appraisal software.

Some appraisers prefer to store images on floppy disk or a removable hard drive system so that images can be easily categorized and filed. The most practical, cost-effective system is a removable hard drive system because it has a fairly large storage capacity and takes up much less space than a floppy disk collection.

APPRAISER'S TIP

To determine if the speed of a color printer is acceptable, add up the number of picture pages in a typical report and multiply the sum by the number of copies typically requested and the number of minutes required to print one page. If this figure is too high, either a faster printer must be selected or the appraiser should wait until faster printing capability is available.

Hardware

For the typical appraiser, the primary concerns regarding digital imaging will be ease of installation, the difficulty and time needed to process and download images, printing resolution, and the cost of each component of the system, i.e., the imaging board, camera, software, printer, and storage medium. The hardware and software can often be purchased as part of a package with significant discounts from the list price.

Cameras. There are three basic types of digital imaging cameras: the digital still camera, still video, and camcorder. Although costs have been coming down, many appraisers still find these items expensive, especially when added to the purchase price of a good color printer and the large amount of disk storage needed to categorize the images. Not all of the cameras have wide-angle or telephoto lenses and few provide a flash for dark interiors. The advantages and disadvantages of each type of camera are outlined in Table 3.1.

Image capture boards. Selecting an image capture board is one of the most inconvenient aspects of a digital imaging system. The capture board, which the appraiser installs in the computer, allows images to be downloaded directly from the computer into the software. Problems

Table 3.1—Imaging Cameras

CAMERA TYPE	EXAMPLES	ADVANTAGES	DISADVANTAGES
Digital Still Camera	Dycam 3XL (B & W) Dycam 4XL (Color) Logitech Fotoman Plus (B & W) Logitech Fotoman Pixtura (Color) Apple Quicktake	Easy to use. No special installation; attaches with its own cable to computer port. Least expensive option. No extra board required for computer.	Quality of image is average. Wide-angle lens adapter required for large buildings. Must download to computer or other storage device after limited number of shots (6-48 depending on model) for desired resolution.
Still Video	Canon RC-360 Canon RC-570	Most professional device. Image quality above average. Stores 50 images on 2-in. removable disks.	Most expensive option. Requires image capture board for computer. Most appraisers need installation assistance.
Camcorder	Any Hi-Eight Model	Least expensive (not including image capture board). Many images per tape.	Requires image capture board and software for computer. Most appraisers need installation assistance. Videotape not a reliable long-term storage medium.

with setting internal switches and installing the board have led many providers to design their software so that a serial port can be used in lieu of the image capture board. The expense and potential inconvenience of an image capture board should be considered when selecting imaging software.

Color printers. The print resolution of the color printer is the weakest component of an imaging system. The maximum resolution varies with the type of printer used and the quality of its components. There are two primary types of color printers. The thermal dye transfer printer, also known as a *color laser printer,* offers the best picture, but it is by far the most expensive to purchase and has the highest cost per page. The inkjet printer is more affordable and offers good picture resolution, although it is noticeably inferior to thermal dye transfer printers. The cost per page is reasonable for most appraisal firms.

Among the factors to evaluate when selecting a color printer for imaging are overall cost, cost per page, quality of text output, print resolution, printer speed, option for network port, technical support, warranty, and payback period.

SUMMARY

Appraisers use a wide variety of devices to assist them in gathering and communicating information. Basic tools such as a camera, clipboard, and measuring wheel or tape are used on every assignment. Many other tools, such as a flashlight, magnet, level, and ice pick, can come in handy depending on the property appraised and the extent of inspection permitted by the property owner. An extra set of clothes and waterproof boots can be useful in inclement weather. Computers and related tools can help streamline the time and effort it takes to complete an appraisal report. Lastly, carrying a calculator, extra batteries, a briefcase, and graph paper is just common sense. Not having a necessary tool will inconvenience the appraiser and the property owner and may even result in an inaccurate appraisal.

CHAPTER 4

SITE INSPECTION

Site inspection is often overlooked in inspection training. As described in *The Appraisal of Real Estate*, "A site is land that is improved so that it is ready to be used for a specific purpose." Improvements may be found on site (e.g., grading, landscaping, paving, utility hookups) and off site (e.g., streets, curbs, sidewalks, drains, connecting utility lines).

Experienced appraisers tend to believe that novices can learn site inspection very quickly because it is easy to see the site's physical features. Ironically, site inspection is frequently mishandled and often causes problems for appraisers, especially when they are called on to appraise vacant land. Site inspection is more than looking at a property. An appraiser must not only see the physical features of a property, but also investigate things that cannot be seen such as flood boundaries and deed restrictions.

Accurate site inspection is also important in discounted cash flow analysis. Many telltale signs of depreciation or potential building problems can be evident from the site inspection. Cracked concrete or problems with asphalt paving may indicate that these site improvements are nearing the end of their useful lives and will require significant expenditures for repair over the holding period. Such factors should be considered in discounted cash flow analysis. Signs of contamination or poor settling of a building may also be discovered in a proper site inspection. These problems are expensive to cure and involve special (usually one-time) expenses that should be factored into a discounted cash flow analysis.[1]

PHYSICAL FEATURES

Many physical features of a site are readily apparent; these include topography, frontage, and paving. Other features such as utilities and water drainage can be difficult to evaluate in an

---

1. Capital improvements to a site or building are deducted after net operating income, but before cash flow. Since appraisers typically capitalize net operating income and not cash flow, these expenses do not affect value. However, to be technically correct, they should be modeled within the cash flow to provide the client with the best analysis possible.

inspection. Unfortunately, many appraisers tend to overlook physical factors and the degree to which they affect the value, use, and marketability of a property. This is especially true in the inspection of comparable sales.

TOPOGRAPHY

The appraiser should observe the topography of a site since this can greatly affect its building potential. It can be more costly, for example, to install site improvements on lots that are not level. Sometimes it is difficult to determine property boundary lines during the inspection or foliage may make it impossible to get to some areas of the site. Although it may be inconvenient for the appraiser to walk the entire site, especially if it contains several acres, not investigating beyond a site's frontage can result in incorrect assumptions and an incorrect value conclusion. The potential for errors grows in sales comparison because few appraisers examine comparable land sales as thoroughly as they examine the subject. If it is not possible or

Figure 4.1—Aerial Photo of Subject and Neighborhhood

practical to walk a site, the appraiser should interview the property owner or discuss the site with another knowledgeable party. Many township engineers are familiar with properties in the community and can provide significant information to appraisers.

Aerial photographs are often helpful in determining the topography and physical features of a site (see Figure 4.1). Although they can be impractical for small properties, they are invaluable for large, multi-acre sites. Because the price of aerial photography has declined significantly, it is often cost-effective and provides additional insight and support. If necessary, the appraiser can build the cost into the appraisal fee up front.

Maps

Maps are important sources of topographical information about a site. Useful maps may include tax maps, floodplain maps, wetlands inventory maps, United States Geological Survey maps, utility maps, soil survey maps, and site plans. Many of these maps can be found at the office of the municipal engineer, planning board, clerk, or assessor.

Tax maps. Tax maps are useful for many reasons. They show a property's boundaries and measurements and help the appraiser visualize the site's shape. Tax maps often show easements that run along or through a property and adjacent properties. Most easements are identified on tax maps, which is important because some easements, such as easements for high-tension power lines, may reduce the marketability and value of a site even if they are not located on the site. Other factors that can affect property value, such as proximity to a landfill, school, or airport, will also be shown. Tax maps may indicate the location of streams, although this practice varies with the municipality and the size of the stream. It is good practice for an appraiser to examine a tax map for every subject and comparable property.

Floodplain maps. Floodplain maps are prepared by the Federal Emergency Management Agency as part of the National Flood Insurance Program. If a property is located within a flood zone, lenders require flood insurance. For this reason, financial institutions require appraisers to report the flood zone designation of a property. Figure 4.2 shows a typical floodplain map.

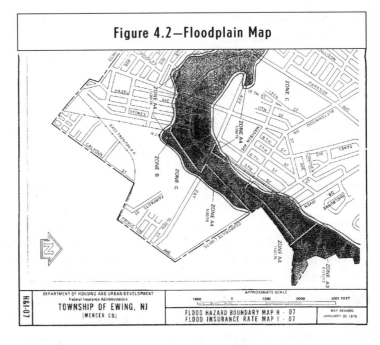

Figure 4.2—Floodplain Map

Most floodplain maps were prepared during the late 1970s and early 1980s. In areas that have not grown much since the map was created, identifying the location of a property on the map is easy. However, it can be very difficult to determine the flood designation of a property in an area that has experienced significant growth. The floodplain maps for highly developed areas often do not show individual lots or newer streets.

Obviously, an appraiser must carefully examine floodplain maps of rural or high-growth areas. Determining the date of the map's last revision is useful because conditions at the property or the flood hazard boundaries may have changed since the map was released. The appraiser should get into the habit of asking the municipal engineer the exact location of the property on the floodplain map. The appraiser should also cite the community panel number (i.e., the number identifying the flood map) and the date of last revision. A copy of the map with an arrow identifying the subject and a sketch showing the boundaries of the site are also desirable.

Floodplain maps are usually available in printed form, although maintaining them for an entire state can be onerous for the appraiser. They are also available on microfiche, which is expensive, and on CD-ROM in some areas. With a CD-ROM the appraiser can easily locate the flood zone classification for a particular property by searching for the address or block and lot number. As technology and applications software continue to develop, CD-ROM will be the preferred medium for future maps.

APPRAISER'S TIP

The appraiser should not blindly accept a tax map as accurate. It is always wise to consult more than one source for lot size, dimensions, and other facts. The site plan, survey, and legal description can be used to verify the accuracy of a tax map. When these sources indicate different measurements, the appraiser should select the most reliable source and qualify the data used with an assumption or limiting condition in the report. It is also a good practice to acknowledge the discrepancy in a prominent section of the report, state which estimate was relied upon, and explain the appraiser's reasoning.

Wetlands inventory maps. As Figure 4.3 illustrates, wetlands inventory maps can be difficult to read. They present an aerial view of a region with the underlying soils colored to represent types and degrees of wetlands. Since properties are not delineated by their lot lines or by municipal classification (e.g., block and lot), it is necessary either to rely on the interpretation of the municipal engineer or to measure the approximate boundaries on the map. This can be accomplished by looking for the nearest cross street on a tax map, measuring the frontages of each lot until the subject is reached, measuring the wetlands map from this cross street, and applying the same frontage reading to the map. (Conversion of scale is usually necessary.) A similar process should be employed to locate the boundaries of the subject on the map.

United States Geological Survey maps. U.S. Geological Survey maps, which show rivers, streams, contours, elevations above sea level, and other physical features, can be valuable in determining the topography of large sites. Such maps can identify sites with grades that make development difficult, expensive, or impossible. Roads are labeled and homes and commercial buildings are indicated. The maps are fairly easy to read, but if they are dated the information will be suspect. Figure 4.4 shows a typical USGS map.

Utility maps. The physical layout of water, sewer, and/or gas lines within a municipality is often drawn on a large municipal map. Since the availability of these utilities can have a major effect on a property's highest and best use, development potential, and value, utility maps can be invaluable. Sometimes the maps indicate future municipal utility expansion, which can also be important. Although these maps are usually too large to copy, the appraiser should, at a

APPRAISER'S TIP

There is more to wetlands than just foliage. A wetlands classification is dependent on three factors: the wetlands map classification, the foliage, and the underlying soil. Many operating farms are situated on wetlands even though no wetlands plants remain. If the underlying soil five or more inches down is classified as wetlands and the map indicates that some form of wetlands is present, the site is classified as wetlands even though this may not be apparent on the surface. Thus, reading a wetlands map and getting an interpretation is critical.

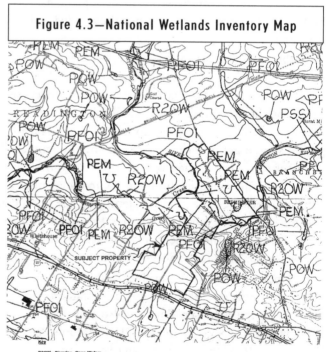

Figure 4.3—National Wetlands Inventory Map

Key
R2OW - Riverine Open Waters
PEM - Palustrine Emergent Wetlands
PFO1 - Palustrine Forested Wetlands

NWI MAP
Nationwide Wetlands Inventory, USF&WS
Block 44, Lots 2.01 & 2.02, .
Bedminster Twp., Somerset County
Block 15, Lots 5, 27 & 29
Readington Township, Hunterdon County, New Jersey

Figure 4.4—U.S. Geological Survey Map

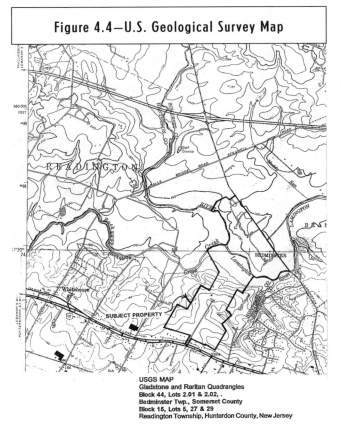

USGS MAP
Gladstone and Raritan Quadrangles
Block 44, Lots 2.01 & 2.02, .
Bedminster Twp., Somerset County
Block 15, Lots 5, 27 & 29
Readington Township, Hunterdon County, New Jersey

Figure 4.5—Septic Map

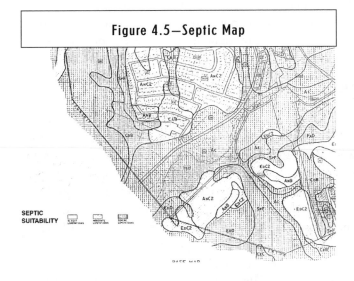

SEPTIC
SUITABILITY

minimum, refer to the maps and the date of their last revision in the appraisal report. If utility maps do not exist for an area, a septic map, which details how suitable the land is for a septic system, may be available. A septic map is shown in Figure 4.5.

Soil survey maps. The U.S. Department of Agriculture has prepared soil survey maps for the entire country. In many parts of the United States, the value of farmland depends on its soil, so appraisers must acquire a thorough working knowledge of soil characteristics. Other facts that can be determined from soil surveys are water table depth and areas of poor drainage. These factors are critical to the development potential of a site, especially when below-grade space is planned. Figure 4.6 depicts a typical soils map.

Site plans. Site plans prepared by an engineering firm are the most site-specific types of maps available. Appraisers should routinely ask property owners for them. Site plans are especially valuable because they are drawn to scale. They include detailed information and often have been prepared more recently than any government map. The location and size of easements, elevations, the building footprint, parking areas, site ingress and egress, detention basins, building setbacks, and accessory site improvements such as dumpster pads, fencing, and concrete curbing can be easily identified. Site plans are extremely important to the appraisal report if the subject property is proposed construction. Because site plans give precise dimensions, they can provide the square foot area of a building that cannot be otherwise measured; this is particularly useful for comparable properties (see Figure 4.7).

Figure 4.6—Soils Map

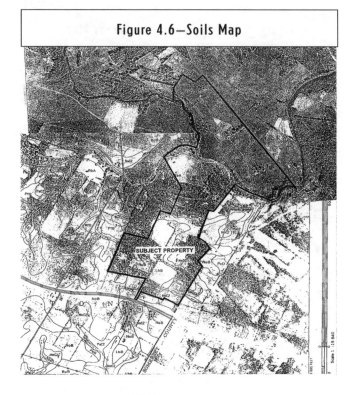

SOILS MAP
Block 44, Lots 2.01 & 2.02, SCSS Sh. No. 10
Bedminster Twp., Somerset County
Block 15, Lots 5, 27 & 29, HCSS Sh. No. 5

Other types of maps. Regional and neighborhood maps, zoning maps, airport noise contour maps, cadastral maps indicating lots and topography, and master land use maps may also prove useful to the appraiser.

FRONTAGE, LOT SIZE, AND LOT DIMENSIONS

The value of a property can depend heavily on its frontage, and substandard frontage can become a highest and best use issue. Many appraisers assume the frontage listed on tax maps is completely accurate, which may not be the case. A tax map may indicate sufficient frontage to meet zoning requirements, but a legal description may provide contradictory evidence. Since most clients request that the legal description of the subject property, which is usually found in the deed, be included in the report, the appraiser should get into the habit of comparing the dimensions on the tax map with the legal description. Frontage and dimensions can also be found on a survey map. When there are significant differences, the appraiser should obtain other opinions or use a site plan as additional support for his or her frontage conclusion. The appraiser should also reconcile any differences in the report and provide a discussion of his or her reasoning.

Lot size and zoning restrictions determine the building area of a site. Excess land, which is not necessary to support the principal improvement, can be subdivided from the site. The location of the building on the lot can be significant because the maximum building coverage (based on zoning) and the distance of the building from the lot lines determines if the building can accommodate expansion.

Familiarity with basic geometry is important in determining lot size. Many software programs can calculate lot size based on a legal description, the dimensions given in a tax map, or an appraiser's estimates.

The shape of a site is important to its development. Sometimes a building must be positioned sideways or on an angle from the road because of the site's shape. It may be difficult to design a building that provides a sufficient yield to warrant development on an irregularly shaped site. Parking on such a lot can also be a problem.

Most municipalities have zoning laws. If a site does not meet all the zoning requirements because of an irregular shape, a

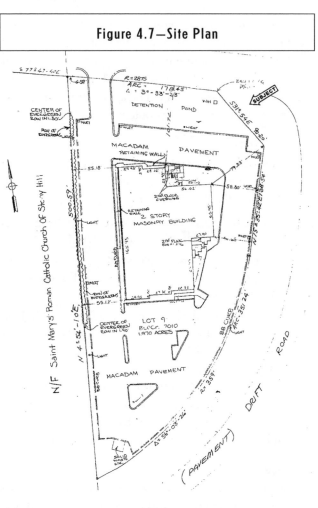

Figure 4.7—Site Plan

variance must be obtained before it can be developed. In this case, the appraiser must use judgment to decide if the variance can be obtained and what effect it will have on value. Discussion with the zoning officer is important. The appraiser should cite the name of the official contacted as well as the date and outcome of any such conversation in case the situation should change after the date of value. The appraiser should also consider any past zoning trends that allowed variances for nonconforming lots.

UTILITIES

Municipal Utilities

The location, amount, and type of municipal utilities are important to the highest and best use of a property and its value. In many instances, all municipal utilities are available in a neighborhood, but some home owners elect to remain on private water or septic systems. The availability of utilities and their installation at the subject should be discussed with the proper municipal authorities, and the persons spoken to should be identified in the report.

Water Quality

If a property has municipal water, the water quality should be acceptable because water supplies are strictly regulated and tested. However, the appraiser should not assume a hazardous condition could not exist. Most problems do not originate with the water supply, but rather with the interior fixtures and the piping into the building. Water intake pipes for many older buildings are made entirely of lead, and some buildings have faucets manufactured with lead. An excessive concentration of sodium may be present in drinking water if a water softener is used. Both of these conditions can be hazardous. The only way to determine if a problem exists is to have the water tested by a laboratory. The appraiser is not responsible for this testing, but it is always best to take note of a potential problem with a limiting condition in the report.

Septic Systems

Several problems may relate to septic systems. As an area makes the transition from septic systems to municipal sewers, older septic systems can be perceived by the market as function-ally obsolete. The location of the system is crucial.

- Septic systems should be located away from a well or driveway for obvious reasons. This is rarely a problem, but it may occur.

- Septic systems should have a slope so that gravity can displace the waste evenly. When the grade is insufficient, waste will clog the system and back up, causing a problem for the home owner.

- The soil should be suitable for a septic field. This can be determined by examining a soil map or discussing the site with knowledgeable municipal officials. Some soils are not suitable for septic systems.

When septic systems fail, the property will usually have wet areas. Lush grass may grow on effluent that has risen to the surface. This section of grass will remain green even after the weather turns cold and the rest of the lawn turns brown. An odor may be noticeable. A common cause of septic system failure is neglect. The home owner may have failed to clean the sludge from the septic tank or the trap that collects waste disposal grease.

Drainage

Problems with drainage include areas of pooled water with or without wetlands plants, problems with detention and retention basins, and water marks on the exterior of a building. These can be costly to fix. Readers of appraisal reports are very interested in drainage prob-lems. Although the property owner will be the primary source of information, neighbors may also know if a problem exists.

Many municipal codes require new commercial buildings to have detention basins. Detention basins are frequently required because building and parking areas are impervious, preventing rainwater from running off into the ground and natural aquifers underneath. Without a detention basin or a drainage plan, runoff will often collect in unwanted places and may even accumulate on adjacent properties after severe storms. As a general rule, each square foot of land area should be able to retain two inches of water.

Inspection. The drainage of a site is often difficult to determine. Although newer development projects usually have detention basins, older sites rarely do. If the land slopes downward toward buildings, the appraiser may have to look for subtle clues to determine the drainage of the site.

Evidence of basement flooding is the most obvious clue that drainage is inadequate. The problem may be caused by surface water draining from higher points on the site toward the building, which eventually seeps into basement areas. Basement flooding can also be caused by septic system failure or subsurface water leakage from a high water table. (A surprising number of older buildings were built on sites with high water tables.) When water is seen seeping from a hill or nearby marshlands, this may indicate a point where the water table extrudes from the ground. The appraiser should suspect a high water table if any of these conditions exist. Installing a curtain drain around the building's perimeter will cure the problem.

If the site slopes toward the building and water collects along its perimeter or at a doorway, the property has a drainage problem. To correct it, the affected area must be landscaped differently.

If a stream is located on or adjacent to the site, the potential for flooding exists. If the stream becomes clogged with debris or fallen trees and a heavy rain occurs, even a tiny brook can create a surface runoff problem. This may or may not affect any buildings on the site, depending on the grade between the banks of the stream and the structures. Evidence of erosion indicates a drainage problem. Where the bank is steep enough, a retaining wall may have been constructed. If the members of an existing wall are bowed or cracks have developed in the mortar, the retaining wall should be mended.

A pond of water on a lawn may or may not be evidence of poor drainage. The appraiser should evaluate its potential to affect the building on the site and find out where the water came from (e.g., from a break in a water line, a sewer system backup, or a heavy rainfall).

PAVING
Both asphalt and concrete paving can cause problems and will require careful observation during the site inspection.

Asphalt
Some common problems with asphalt paving have rather comical names—i.e., alligatoring, lunch breaks, and bird baths. Other problems include potholes, undulating surfaces, oil and grease stains, variable seal coatings, and the fading of surface markings in parking areas.

Alligatoring. The most common asphalt problem is *alligatoring,* which is defined as cracks in the surface layer of materials only, which widen from contraction caused by a sudden change in temperature, lack of binder, insufficient drying time between coats, poor penetration, or applying a hard film over a soft undercoat.[2]

Although alligatoring is usually associated with a simple crack in the paving, it can also be a soft spot in a parking area which develops numerous small cracks that grow over time. There is no particular pattern of cracks, but fault lines will often appear in the pavement. Cracks tend to develop in areas that receive a high volume of automobile and truck traffic. If not repaired, they eventually will turn into potholes.

Lunch breaks. A *lunch break* is a crack that forms at the intersection of two areas of asphalt paving, usually where an older section meets a newer one (see Figure 4.8). Lunch breaks are created when a joint between two surfaces is filled in improperly. These types of cracks are not common, but they are a problem nonetheless.

Bird baths. A *bird bath* is "a concavity in a pavement surface which holds water after a shower or rain."[3] *Ponding* is another name for this type of problem, which is common in surface parking areas. Bird baths are usually caused by improper grading and paving. When a crack develops, surface water leaks into it and, if the water freezes, the crack will expand and eventually result in a pothole. If bird baths are located away from heavy traffic areas, they do

---

2. National Association of Women in Construction, *Construction Dictionary,* 8th ed. (Phoenix: National Association of Women in Construction, Greater Phoenix Arizona Chapter #98, 1991), 18.

3. Ibid., 58.

not pose much of a problem. However, they are often forerunners of alligatoring in high-traffic areas. Figure 4.9 shows a bird bath.

Other defects. Less serious asphalt paving problems include the fading of striping, arrows, and designated fire lane markings in parking areas. Variable seal coatings and oil and grease stains are not a problem, but they indicate gradual deterioration. Undulating surfaces can create a problem over time if cracks develop. Speed bumps can be a mixed blessing. Because they slow traffic, they reduce potholes but, in areas where it snows, speed bumps can be greatly damaged by snowplows. Potholes can be patched, but this almost never cures the problems due to excessive wear and the freezing/thawing process.

CONCRETE

Although most people think concrete is impervious, it does absorb some water. As with asphalt paving, water causes cracks to expand in freezing temperatures. The structural problems that affect concrete are harder to notice. The steel mesh used to reinforce concrete can rust due to water penetration and eventually destroy the integrity of the concrete. Other problems relate to the control joints—i.e., the spaces between blocks of sidewalk cement—and to the progressive growth of tree roots underneath. Control joints, which help control concrete expansion and contraction, may be spaced too far apart. Concrete problems are expensive to fix. Common concrete paving defects include spalling, cracking, wide separations, sinking, heaving, and cavitation.

Figure 4.8—Lunch Break

Figure 4.9—Bird Bath or Ponding

Cracking and spalling. The most common problem affecting concrete is cracking, caused primarily by underground tree roots pushing up the concrete. Cracks can be filled, but if the underlying problem is not corrected, cracks will reappear. Concrete is also susceptible to heaving, sinking, and cavitation, which is similar to bird baths in asphalt paving. These problems are fairly obvious (see Figure 4.10).

Spalling, the cracking or flaking of surface particles, is evidenced by small concrete chips on top of the paved area (see Figure 4.11).

HAZARDOUS CONDITIONS

Hazardous conditions can include environmental contamination, sinkholes created by developers who bury debris and then build over it, and flooding from natural springs near the surface. Although hazardous conditions are often difficult to detect, the appraiser has the responsibility to note any unusual conditions. Some hazardous conditions may indicate the need for inspections by other professionals. There are five primary sources for information on the existence of hazardous conditions.

Figure 4.10—Sinking and Cracking Concrete

Figure 4.11—Spalling Concrete

1. The local assessor, especially one who has had a long tenure in office, is usually familiar with the area and knows whether a hazardous condition could or does exist. If the appraiser needs to visit the assessor's office, asking one additional question is rarely troublesome.

2. The property owner is often a reliable source for information on hazardous conditions. However, the appraiser should be aware that the owner may be biased and not reveal that such conditions exist.

3. Local residents, especially neighbors, are usually aware of hazardous conditions because they are often affected by them. Most neighbors will gladly volunteer such information when the appraiser asks.

4. Building inspectors often know of hazardous conditions on a site or in a building and they will readily supply this information.

5. Newspapers publish information on hazardous conditions, which may be front page news in local papers.

The appraiser is not obligated to contact all these sources but, at the very least, he or she should question the assessor and property owner and state this in the appraisal

APPRAISER'S TIP

The Appraisal Institute's Property Observation Checklist can be useful in the appraiser's site inspection. The checklist represents a limited scope analysis which can be used to support the appraiser's conclusions about the site. The complete checklist appears in the appendix.

report. This effort could substantially limit the appraiser's liability on this sensitive issue.

Underground Storage Tanks

The presence and condition of underground tanks can be very difficult to ascertain during an inspection. Newer fiberglass tanks pose little threat, but older metal tanks are subject to corrosion and decay.

Problems with underground tanks, most notably oil storage tanks, have become prevalent in recent years. If contamination is present, it can cost thousands or even tens of thousands of dollars to remediate. To correct the problem, a specialized environmental cleanup company must be engaged to remove the soil surrounding the tank as well as the tank itself. If a nearby aquifer has been contaminated, litigation can last for years. If an underground tank is present on a site and a valid certification is not in place, a certain percentage of the market may not be interested in the property, its value may be negatively impacted, and the marketing time could be lengthened. The effect on property value will depend on the number of such properties in the area and market preferences.

Inspection. The appraiser should ask the local assessor, fire marshal, and/or building department if there are any underground tanks on the site. If the building is heated with oil, a tank will probably be found in the basement or outside; otherwise, the appraiser can assume an underground oil tank is buried nearby. Some type of access cover will usually be visible at ground level.

The property owner should be questioned about underground tanks. However, the owner may be reluctant to reveal any potential problem and the appraiser should not consider this source of information reliable. In any case, the appraiser should prominently state in the report that he or she attempted to consult the owner regarding the presence of underground tanks. If no attempt is made and a problem exists, the appraiser will be negligent and incur significant business risk.

If a tank is present, the appraiser should determine if it is made of steel and when it was buried. Steel tanks are generally good for 20 years, but they can rust sooner if neglected. Homes converted to gas heat may still have oil tanks buried on the premises. A neglected tank could pose an environmental hazard.

OTHER FACTORS

In addition to physical factors, less tangible factors such as deed and airplane overflight restrictions can affect the usability and value of a site.

DEED RESTRICTIONS

A deed restriction is "a limitation that passes with the land regardless of the owner; [it] usually limits the real estate's type of use or intensity of use."[4] Deed restrictions may or may not be recorded. For example, covenants, conditions, and restrictions (CC&Rs) frequently apply to residential subdivisions, but they are not found on deeds. When deed restrictions are not public information, the appraiser is not liable if they are overlooked; when they are recorded, however, the appraiser is fully liable. Appraisers should get into the habit of reading the most recent deed, at the very least. The following limiting condition, which appears in virtually every appraisal report, helps limit the appraiser's liability.

> The appraiser has not considered and assumes no responsibility for the legal description or for legal matters. The title to the property is assumed to be good and marketable and the property is appraised free and clear of any or all liens or encumbrances unless stated otherwise.

ADJACENT LAND USES

The properties adjacent to or near the subject property can have an impact on its value. If a property is next to a landfill, incinerator, or other potential hazard, its marketability and value can be dramatically reduced. Even uses several blocks away can result in lower property values. For example, proximity to an airport or train lines creates noise and ground vibrations that can reduce property values throughout the area.

Property owners are reluctant to give information on nearby nuisances because they risk a lower appraised value. Appraisers may fail to notice train tracks behind foliage or sloping topography; similarly, airplanes may not fly over the subject property during the inspection. Such factors can easily be overlooked. Discussions with municipal officials that are documented in the report will limit the appraiser's liability.

SUMMARY

An appraiser must be concerned with many details when performing a site inspection. The site's topography, drainage, frontage, lot size and dimensions, shape, utilities, and other physical characteristics affect its value. Sources of information can include various types of maps, site plans, and other documents. Problems with septic systems, water quality, and underground tanks can have a negative impact on the marketability, development potential, and value of a site. The appraiser must be aware of these factors, make use of the data sources available, assess the functional adequacy of the site, and properly consider the value impact of any problems found.

---

4. Appraisal Institute. *The Dictionary of Real Estate Appraisal,* 3d ed. (Chicago: Appraisal Institute, 1993), 91.

CHAPTER 5

HOME INSPECTION

The appraisal of residential properties requires good inspection skills. Property inspection is the foundation for the selection of comparable sales and the quantification of adjustments in the sales comparison approach. Cost approach data derived in the inspection include estimates of the property's effective age, accrued depreciation, functional obsolescence, and external obsolescence. Quality of construction is also evaluated, which facilitates the selection of appropriate cost-estimating data. The physical condition of the property is used to judge the reasonableness of expense estimates developed in the income capitalization approach. Of course, the overwhelming majority of residential appraisals rely on the sales comparison approach only, and a thorough inspection is crucial.

PREPARING TO INSPECT

PRELIMINARY TASKS

The period before the inspection is a time of organization and planning. The following list indicates important tasks to be completed prior to the inspection.

1. The appraiser should contact the municipality where the property is located. Many municipalities have part-time personnel in one or more departments. Since the appraiser will need information from several individuals, including at

least the assessor, the municipal engineer, and the zoning officer, knowing the days and times when these officials are available will make the appraiser's field work more efficient. The appraiser should also verify where these officials work—i.e., at the municipal building, in county buildings, or out of their homes (usually in rural areas). This is especially important when the subject is located far away. Getting key information the first time will save an extra trip.

2. The property owner should be contacted to arrange a date and time to inspect the subject property. During this initial contact, the appraiser should ask for documentation to better understand the building and the site. The appraiser should ask for copies of the building plans, site plan, deeds, and lease agreements, if available. At the very least, the appraiser will review most of these items and include photocopies of them in the addenda to the appraisal report. The appraiser should leave his or her name and telephone number with the owner in case the appointment must be canceled.

3. A search through local multiple listing service (MLS) data should be made for recent sales and listings of properties similar to the subject. If the owner has already been contacted, his or her description of the subject property can help the appraiser select appropriate listing and sale comparables from the MLS. The MLS is also a verification source since the listing broker and perhaps the selling brokers will be identified. Note that estimates of square footage may be missing or inaccurate. The size of the comparable homes should be verified with the assessor, the building department, or persons involved in the transactions.

4. A search through other data sources such as TRW-REDI or Metroscan may be worthwhile. Most appraisers obtain their comparable sales information from such providers, but information on prior sales of the subject may also be available.

5. The appraiser should get all the necessary forms and tools together for the inspection. Most or all of these items can be permanently stored in the trunk of the car so they are available when the appraiser needs them.

MUNICIPAL INVESTIGATIONS

As mentioned in Chapter 4, municipal officials have valuable information for appraisers. The appraiser will need to gather information from several departments.

Assessor's Office

The assessor's office maintains property record cards and has information on assessments, tax rates, tax ratios, and recent comparable sales. The assessor should also have answers to hard questions regarding the ownership history of the subject, any past contamination, the presence of underground tanks, any stigma associated with the property, and negative influences in the neighborhood. The assessor can often tell the appraiser things that he or she would be unable to determine without the cooperation of the owner —e.g., the functional layout of the interior, the type of heat, the amount of electrical service, the existence of private deed restrictions. Usually an interior inspection of the comparable sales is not possible and facts that affected their sale prices often can only be obtained from the assessor. Although the assessor is a good source of information, his or her time may be limited. There are other sources of information that the appraiser can use to obtain similar information.

Property record cards contain a large amount of useful information: the layout of the home; its date of construction; the number of bedrooms and bathrooms; the type of plumbing, electrical, and heating systems present; general building construction information such as the roof type and degree of finish in the basement or attic (if any); and the location of ancillary structures on the property such as a detached garage, shed, or pool. Some states make property record cards public, while others do not. In areas where they are classified as public information, large data providers regularly scan key details or entire property records and make them available to the public for a fee. It may be cost-effective for the appraiser to subscribe to this service. In areas where property record cards are private, an assessor may agree to provide one or more property record cards to an appraiser as a professional courtesy.

Zoning Office

The local zoning officer has a zoning map and information on zoning ordinances that pertain to the subject. Many clients require that a copy of the zoning ordinances be included somewhere in the report, usually in the addenda. The zoning officer may also know if the subject is in compliance with current zoning ordinances and how well the building meets current demands. The appraiser should always verify the current zoning and the validity of the zoning ordinances. If the subject is a legal, nonconforming use, the zoning officer can confirm this. It is also worthwhile to ask if there are any plans to change the zoning or if a new master plan will be adopted.

Building Department

The building department or township engineer will know if a building has a history of code violations or other structural problems. Neighbors with complaints about an adjoining building often go to the building department. The officials may have an idea of what it would cost to bring the property up to current code, as evidenced by the renovation costs incurred to upgrade similar properties. They may also know in what ways the property does not meet the current code. They will be aware of trends in the construction materials used and in electrical and plumbing requirements. However, building department officials cannot be expected to assess market perceptions and values changes; this is the appraiser's job.

The municipal engineer maintains important maps which appraisers should reference. At the very least, floodplain maps are available and most clients specifically require the flood designation of a property to be included in the appraisal. Although the property record card may not be available to the public, the engineer will usually have plans that show the layout, square footage, and other characteristics of the subject property. Also available from the engineer are topographical maps, soil maps, utility maps, wetlands maps, and others, free for the asking.

Building plans are usually available at the engineer's office upon request, although they may be difficult to view if they are older and have been transcribed onto microfilm. In highly developed urban areas where property record cards are unavailable and buildings abut one another, it may be virtually impossible to measure the side and rear dimensions of a building. Viewing the building plans at the engineer's office may be the only way to get accurate square footage measurements of the subject and comparable sales.[1]

Appraiser's Tip

Be careful when examining and relying on building plans. Developers may not construct a building to the exact size specified in the plans. The appraiser should make it a policy always to measure the subject property. The building may have received an addition after the plans were drawn, so measurement of the subject is always warranted.

---

1. When relying on building plans, the appraiser should reference them within the appraisal. The name and address of the company that prepared the plans should be mentioned along with the date the plans were last revised and the job number.

In some urban areas of the country, Sanborn Building and Property Altas maps from Real Estate Data, Inc. may be available. These are similar to large tax maps which show the lot dimensions and building perimeters within the lots. An appraiser can determine the size of a building by determining the scale of the drawing, measuring the sides of the building on the map with an engineer's rule, and then converting these measurements into building dimensions. Commercial properties are typically found on these maps and some residential properties may be outlined. Sanborn Insurance maps, if available, are usually found at the engineer's office or at the county tax board.

Water and Sewer Departments

Water and sewer departments can provide information on the availability of these utilities and any plans to expand lines or capacity. They will know if the property owner is delinquent in utility payments. This may be a sign of cash flow problems. Obviously, this information is important to a client and should be included within the report.

Tax Collector

The tax collector should be consulted for the current tax status of the property. If there are outstanding tax liens, the tax collector can calculate the principal and interest due as of the date of value. Although standard assumptions and limiting conditions state that the property is appraised without regard to liens or title considerations, this information is useful to a potential lender. If taxes have not been paid, this should be noted in the report.

Township Clerk

The township clerk often serves as a central clearinghouse for information, making photocopies of tax maps, zoning ordinances, and other documents in lieu of the respective departments. In small municipalities, the clerk is often the only full-time official who can provide this information. Part-time municipal officials may give important zoning ordinances or public sale records to the clerk, who is regularly available to the public.

Other Departments

Other municipal departments consulted less frequently may include the planning board (for the status of approvals), the affordable housing office, and the rent control board. The planning office at the county or municipal level often has valuable information. It frequently maintains the most up-to-date land use maps. Planning officials know if plans have been filed for future property uses which may compete with the subject. The department can also be a repository for feasibility studies, research reports, environmental impact studies, and other hard-to-obtain professional analyses which have a direct impact on the subject.

The recorder of deeds and mortgages at the county level is another important source of information. It is standard operating procedure for appraisers to consider all sales of the subject transacted within one year for residential property and three years for commercial properties. When neither the property owner nor the assessor can make a deed available, the county recorder will have it. An appraiser can search for a chain of title easily by obtaining the most recent deed and noting if there are any references to a prior sale transaction. Deeds usually cite the prior seller's name and the deed book and page where the transaction is recorded. This makes it easy to determine the ownership history of the subject.

It is common practice to include a legal description within the appraisal report. The easiest way to obtain the legal description is to acquire the last recorded deed and to include it in the addenda to the report. The county deed and mortgage repository may also have tax maps when they are not available at municipal offices.

The county assessor's office or county tax board can be a valuable source of information. Often it is the best place to start developing comparable sales data because all public sale information for every municipality in the county is available. Driving from town to town to locate comparable sales is inefficient, especially when sales information for each town can be found at the tax board. Tax boards are located within the county complex. Since the appraiser must usually go to the repository of deeds and mortgages to obtain a copy of the prior deed or research the chain of title, tax boards are conveniently located. The state tax board may be the only source for public information if there are no assessors at the municipal level and no local property record cards. County tax boards usually have tax maps that can be photocopied as well as the tax rolls for all the municipalities in the county.

OTHER SOURCES OF INFORMATION

In addition to municipal officials, the appraiser may wish to contact other knowledgeable persons for their insights. If local or regional newspapers have run negative stories about a property, a possible stigma may be attached to it and this would result in a lower value and a longer marketing period. Local utility companies often have current information on events in the area or development trends that may affect the subject.

PURPOSE OF BUILDING INSPECTION

In most cases, the appraiser acts as the "eyes and ears" of the client. He or she may be the only independent, impartial person involved in the property transaction. In addition to identifying important property characteristics for the reader of the appraisal, the appraiser looks for telltale signs that a major repair may be necessary. If a defect is overlooked and excluded from the report, the appraiser will provide a faulty appraisal that is not in compliance with the Uniform Standards of Professional Appraisal Practice and may face a negligence lawsuit. The most common repairs to keep in mind when doing an inspection are the replacement of a roof, replacement of plumbing, renovation of the exterior, foundation renovation, repair of the heating and cooling systems, correction of water seepage or termite damage, and electrical system repair.

There is no set order for property inspection. Some appraisers prefer to gather information in the neighborhood, then examine the building exterior, and finish with the interior. Others prefer to go straight to the owner and do the interior inspection first. It is usually best to measure the exterior of the building and then do the interior inspection; this will result in the most accurate sketch of the interior floor plan.

EXTERIOR BUILDING MEASUREMENT

Although measuring the dimensions of a building may seem simple, the process has its share of nuances. The appraiser will need a clipboard, paper, pen or pencil, measuring tape, and perhaps a staking tool or screwdriver. If the assignment is to be completed to meet Fannie Mae guidelines, a plan of each floor must be drawn. For these assignments, it is wise to use graph paper to record exterior measurements so the interior floor plan can be drawn to scale within the outline of the exterior. Obtaining the size of a home from building plans, model brochures, tax assessment records, real estate brokers, or other sources is not an acceptable substitute for the appraiser's actual measurements.

It does not matter where the appraiser begins measuring. Most simply start at the front of the home for convenience. The measuring tape can usually be hooked to one end of an exterior wall and stretched to the opposite end, at which point the appraiser writes down the measurement. When the side to be measured is too long or is obstructed by trees or other objects, a hook staking tool or screwdriver can be used. If heavy snow is present, measurements must be taken further away from the structure. After attaching the measuring tape to a longer tool such as a thin metal stake, the appraiser lines up the tape with the building, stretches it, and takes a reading. Keeping the tape straight to get the most accurate reading, the appraiser repeats the process to measure each side of the structure. Once measurements of the building perimeter are taken, the appraiser should note the location of doors, windows, and overhangs on the sketch. Overhangs can be drawn with dotted lines so that they will not be confused with ground floor measures.[2]

The appraiser should check to see that the measurements for the opposite sides of the building are equal; if not, one or more sides may need to be measured again. To measure gross living area, the home is divided into smaller geometric areas (usually rectangles) and the area of each section is calculated separately. The areas of the sections are then added together to derive gross living area. (The calculation of gross living area is discussed in more detail in a subsequent section of the chapter.)

ADDITIONS

Most additions to a home will be square or rectangular. The appraiser measures each wall of the addition and double checks to see that the opposite sides are equal.

If the area to be measured is circular, it can be difficult to obtain accurate square foot measurements. For a circular area at ground level, the appraiser should start by measuring the outside areas and then measure the radius of the circle from the inside. The gross living area is then calculated using the equation $\pi \times r^2$ (approximately 3.14 times the radius squared). When the area is above grade, as in the case of a circular observatory room or "crow's nest," measuring the interior radius and applying the formula will suffice. Geodesic domes are measured using the same technique. The interior radius is measured and the $\pi \times r^2$ equation is applied.

---

2. Including additional square footage for an overhang when recording building size is a common error noticed by reviewers. The error most often occurs when the appraiser identifies the overhang using the same type of solid line used for the rest of the building and then calculates incorrectly.

EXTERIOR INSPECTION

When inspecting the exterior of a home, the appraiser will generally focus on its location on the lot, its architectural style, and its construction.

The location of the building on the lot can indicate if there is sufficient room for expansion. Depending on the size of the site and the location of the building, there may be sufficient area to subdivide the lot without obtaining a zoning variance; if so, a valuation of the excess land will be necessary. In some areas the direction the building faces is important and the presence of trees that obstruct the sunlight should be noted. In warm climates, nearby trees can help reduce the home's cooling costs; homes in cold climates can have higher heating costs if sunlight is blocked by trees.

The architectural style of a home helps determine its marketability and value. The most important question to consider is whether the architectural style of the home meets market tastes. The home styles found in a neighborhood indicate the acceptance of a particular architectural style. When a home is out of step with the neighborhood—e.g., too large or too modern compared to other homes—a lower value and longer marketing time may result. If a home has had various additions over several decades, its overall style may be incompatible with the market. Quality differences in architectural style can be difficult to judge, especially when a home has had multiple additions. The appraiser must be careful in comparing the architectural style of the subject to other neighborhood improvements because a difference could be an asset if the style is in favor. For instance, the outdated design or unique features of an historic home may actually add to its value.

Another aspect of architectural style is the number of stories in a home. A residence can have a single story, one and one-half stories, two stories, or more than two stories, or it may be a bi-level or split-level. In some parts of the country, split-level homes are considered functionally obsolete and they have longer marketing times as a result. The appraiser should become familiar with market tastes in the area to determine if an architectural style is obsolete. (Common house types are identified in the appendix. The advantages and disadvantages of each type are described.)

The physical construction of the exterior should be examined. This includes the quality and type of roofing, the exterior veneer, the size of the garage, the location of entrances, the condition and type of foundation, the number of chimneys, and the types of windows. All of these items should be evaluated in terms of condition, market desirability, and degree of functional obsolescence.

The appraiser should be familiar with the various elements of residential construction. Available reference materials include the Appraisal Institute's *Appraising Residential Properties,* home construction seminars sponsored by various appraisal societies, and the many books and pamphlets published by the American Society of Home Inspectors.

EXTERIOR SIDING, SHEATHING, AND FLASHING

There are many types of home exteriors. During the inspection the appraiser notes the condition and type of exterior siding, underlying sheathing, and flashing. If properly maintained, siding should have a useful life equal to the life of the home.

The five primary types of exterior siding material and their characteristics are listed in Table 5.1.

Table 5.1—Types and Characteristics of Home Exteriors

MATERIAL	CHARACTERISTICS
Brick veneer	Popular, but losing some appeal due to the rising demand for stucco; requires little maintenance
Stucco (original and synthetic)	Rising in popularity due to increased use of European and contemporary styles; can be quite expensive
Unpainted cedar and other wood	Suits contemporary styles; requires maintenance
Painted wood, pressboard	Traditional material; considered high maintenance, but low cost
Aluminum, vinyl siding	Attractive, low maintenance (up to 50-year warranty), reasonable initial cost

Source: Appraisal Institute, Residential Property Construction and Inspection seminar workbook.

Inspection

Some exterior conditions can be easily observed.

- Walls may be bulging or sagging.

- Cracks in stucco or damaged brick should be noted because they are very expensive to fix. These problems can be caused by settling, nearby trees that scrape against the exterior during storms, or poor workmanship during initial construction. If water gets behind stucco and freezes, its expansion will aggravate the cracks and cause more harm.

- If the subject has a brick exterior, the bricks may not have been glazed or fired properly. Since bricks retain more water than other exteriors, the gradual freezing/thawing process can allow water to penetrate. Interior walls may show water spots as a result. This condition is expensive to fix.

- The mortar used for brick siding may deteriorate due to foundation settling. This can allow moisture to penetrate the structure. Cracks should be sealed.

- Missing wood or cedar shingles and damaged siding are also apparent. Shingles may be cracked, rotted, or chipped. It is important to note these deficiencies because moisture or rain will be absorbed if the underlying sheathing is not sufficiently waterproof. If this is the case, the affected portion of the wooden frame and interior walls may suffer over time.

- The southern or southwestern sides of the home will show the most deterioration due to the continuous effects of the sun and the resulting temperature changes.

- If blisters and peeling are evident in the exterior paint, the underlying wood may show signs of moisture penetration.

- If the siding is aluminum, scratches on the finish are not a problem because aluminum does not rust. Aluminum siding should be grounded because it conducts electricity; this is usually accomplished with a wire connecting the siding to a rod affixed to the ground.

- Vinyl siding may show signs of waving or sagging due to poor nailing and workmanship.

- Damage to flashing—i.e., the strips of metal nailed to the intersections of the sheathing and the foundation or roof—should be noted.

- Vines on the outside of a home can pose a problem because their roots can create openings for moisture and water penetration. The appraiser should be alert for interior water spots.

Other potential problems may be less obvious. For example, the condition of the underlying sheathing can be difficult to determine because the exterior material is installed over it. The appraiser can use a screwdriver to peer underneath shingles, noting any potential problems. Or the appraiser can look where the siding ends along corners to observe the condition of the underlying sheathing.

ROOFING

The appraiser will need to examine the roofing material, the slope of the roof, and its condition.

Material

There are many types of roofing material. They vary tremendously in their cost, applicability in various parts of the country, durability, and market acceptance. Table 5.2 shows common types of roofing and their features.

Slope

The slope of the roof and the roofing material are important in determining its desirability and expected useful life. A flat roof can be a problem for a home owner because water will pond. Flat roofs also require more expensive materials and more labor than simple, asphalt-shingle gable roof. A flat roof is subject to more air bubbles, tears, and general abuse than a gable roof. These problems become aggravated as water expands and contracts, often penetrating the underlying layers and causing internal problems. Moreover, ventilation can be a problem; moss or other plants may grow where the roof cover has been compromised and their roots can penetrate the outer roof layer.

Styles

In addition to providing basic protection from the elements, a roof can help characterize the style of a home. There are seven basic styles of roofs (i.e., flat, shed, gable, saltbox, gambrel, hip, and mansard) and many hybrids of two or more styles. Flat roofs are common for commercial properties, but rarely seen on homes. Many home buyers perceive a flat roof to have more problems. The shed roof, which has a slight downward slope from the rear to the front, is fairly common on older homes. The gable roof, with a pitched center and two sloping sides, is the dominant roof style. The saltbox roof, which resembles a hybrid of the gable roof on the upper story and a shed roof on the lower level, is most common in the Northeast. Less common roof styles include the gambrel, reminiscent of the roofs seen on old barns; the hip roof, which is similar to a gable but with half the slope; and the mansard roof, which is similar to a hip roof but with a veneer extension which overhangs most or all of the sides. All these roof types are depicted in Figure 5.1. If the roof style is atypical for the neighborhood and the market perceives it to be unattractive, it may be functionally obsolete and have a negative impact on value.

Inspection

Telltale signs of roof deterioration are described below.

- Curled, peeling, or discolored roof tiles may be due to gradual weathering or nearby trees that scrape the roof, especially during a storm. Shingles that are curled, broken, or cracked allow water to leak in, which can undermine the integrity of the roof deck.

Table 5.2—Roof Types and Characteristics

ROOF TYPE	LIFE EXPECTANCY	CHARACTERISTICS
Asphalt shingles*	15-20 years	Used on approximately 80% of all residential roofs; requires little maintenance
Asphalt mullet-thickness shingles*	20-30 years	Heavier and more durable than regular asphalt shingles
Asphalt interlocking shingles*	15-25 years	Especially good in high wind areas
Asphalt rolls	10 years	Used on low-sloping roofs
Built-up roofing	10-20 years	Used on low-sloping roofs; 2 to 3 times more expensive than asphalt shingles
Wood shingles*	10-40 years†	Must be treated with preservative every 5 years to prevent decay; outlawed in California due to flammability although they are quite fire-resistant
Clay tiles*	20+ years	Durable, fireproof, but not watertight; requires a good subsurface base
Cement tiles*	20+ years	Same characteristics as clay tiles
Slate shingles*	30-100 years‡	Extremely durable, but brittle and expensive
Asbestos cement shingles* (no longer available)	30-75 years	Durable, but brittle and difficult to repair; hazardous material
Metal roofing	15-40 years	Comes in sheets and shingles; should be well grounded for protection from lightning; certain metals must be painted
Single-ply membrane	15-25 years (manufacturer's claim)	New material, has not yet passed the test of time

* Not recommended for use on low-sloping roofs
† Depends on local conditions and proper installation
‡ Depends on quality of slate
Source: American Society of Home Inspectors, "All About Roofs" brochure.

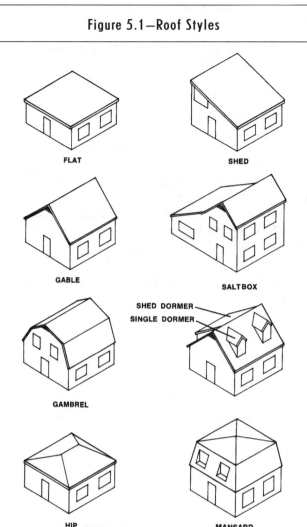

Figure 5.1—Roof Styles

FLAT

SHED

GABLE

SALTBOX

SHED DORMER
SINGLE DORMER

GAMBREL

HIP

MANSARD

Courtesy of Henry S. Harrison, *Houses-The Illustrated Guide to Construction, Design & Systems,* 2d ed. (Chicago: Residential Sales Council of the Realtors National Marketing Institute, 1992).

- A roof that is uneven could indicate unsatisfactory installation of a layer of the roof or warped decking underneath. A bowed or sagging roof usually signals a structural problem.

- If possible, the appraiser should look in the gutters for an accumulation of roof pebbles; this is often the first sign that a roof is deteriorating. Since asphalt shingles have pebbles affixed to them to reflect ultraviolet light, the loss of these pebbles will allow ultraviolet rays to curl the shingles and eventually a new roof will be needed. Usually, the southern side of the roof, which faces the sun, will show the most deterioration. If a third or more of the roof has damaged, curling, or missing roof tiles, it is time to replace that side of the roof. This should be prominently mentioned in the appraisal.

- Moss may be visible on wood and built-up roofs. As the roots of the moss expand, water may penetrate the underlying layer. Moss also curls the adjacent shingles and should be removed.

- Damage to the soffit, the underlayer of the roof, often indicates problems to come.

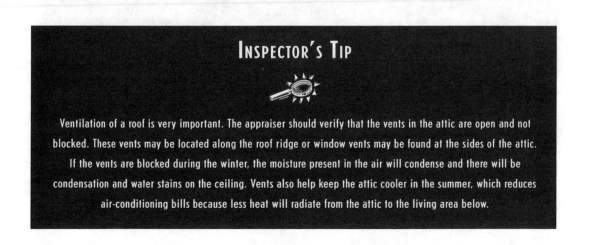

INSPECTOR'S TIP

Ventilation of a roof is very important. The appraiser should verify that the vents in the attic are open and not blocked. These vents may be located along the roof ridge or window vents may be found at the sides of the attic. If the vents are blocked during the winter, the moisture present in the air will condense and there will be condensation and water stains on the ceiling. Vents also help keep the attic cooler in the summer, which reduces air-conditioning bills because less heat will radiate from the attic to the living area below.

APPRAISER'S TIP

If the subject has a flat roof, the appraiser can simply walk around it to determine its structural integrity and amount of deterioration. The appraiser should proceed with caution because, if the deck underneath is wooden and has deteriorated, it is possible that walking on it could cause a hole and possible injury. It is best to inspect a pitched roof from the ground using binoculars. The condition of the roof can also be ascertained from an interior inspection of the attic. Signs of leakage and other problems may be evident only from the inside.

- Damage to the fascia, the rafters that extend out to the edge of the roof, also can create problems in the future.

- The appraiser should look at the joints where the roof meets the piping and chimneys and at the ridge where the sides of a pitched roof meet. The first signs of deterioration often appear here.

- If the roof is flat, note the areas of water ponding. Where water ponds, fungi and plants can grow and their roots can puncture the covering, allowing water to seep into the lower level. If this water then freezes, it will expand the hole and the problem. Any cracks in the roof cover should be sealed to prevent water penetration. Blisters and air bubbles should be noted. The perimeter of the roof and the joints where the walls meet the roof should be closely examined for cracks and punctures to the roof membrane.

- The appraiser should ask the owner when the roof was last repaired or when a new roof was installed. A simple question can save a lot of problems later on.

DOORS AND WINDOWS

Doors have solid or hollow cores and are typically made of wood, metal, or glass. They vary in energy efficiency and durability. Metal doors are preferred in high-crime areas where a wooden door may be functionally obsolete. Glass windows in doors are a security concern. The glass can easily be broken and an intruder can reach through to open the lock on the inside. Locks on doors also vary. Standard locks are the most vulnerable followed by deadbolt locks; two-

APPRAISER'S TIP

If the subject is under an agreement of sale, the appraiser can reduce his or her business risk tremendously with a single technique. It is common to find one or more paragraphs in the agreement which recommend that the buyer have the dwelling inspected and evaluated by a qualified inspector to identify physical defects or environmental conditions. The appraiser should cite this passage or at least make mention of it in the appraisal. The appraiser can also make the appraisal subject to a satisfactory report regarding radon testing and termite inspection from a qualified contractor, engineer, or building inspector. If such a study has been completed prior to finishing the appraisal, a copy can be requested and included in the addenda to the report. Even if the subject is not under contract, the appraiser should ask the owner to request studies from these experts to help limit business risk. If studies are not made available, the appraiser should state in the report that he or she requested them from the owner.

Figure 5.2—Types of Interior Doors

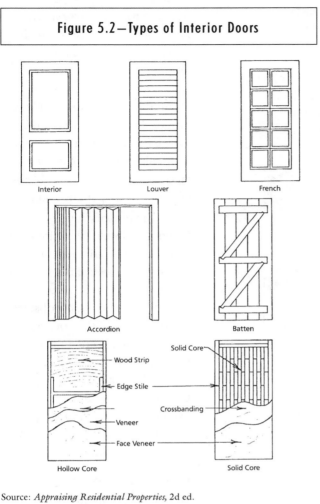

Interior   Louver   French

Accordion   Batten

Wood Strip
Edge Stile
Veneer
Face Veneer
Hollow Core

Solid Core
Crossbanding
Solid Core

Source: *Appraising Residential Properties,* 2d ed.
(Chicago: Appraisal Institute, 1994.)

sided key entry systems are the safest. The presence or absence of weatherstripping on doors should be observed. Figure 5.2 shows typical door types.

Windows come in many types and designs, some of which are shown in Figure 5.3. The appraiser should note whether the windows are single- or double-hung, if any panes are cracked or broken, and if the windows are glazed to increase energy efficiency. The type of frame is also important, with wood, aluminum, and steel being the most common. Wooden windows can eventually rot and in many older homes have been replaced with aluminum. Steel windows are vulnerable to rust. Evidence of cracking in the corners of a window indicate stress-bearing problems which should be noted. Storm windows are important for homes in cold climates.

GARAGES

Garages are easy to inspect because they are fairly standardized in terms of style and finish. The appraiser is primarily concerned with the type of garage (e.g., carport, detached or attached), the number and type of garage doors, the overall design and condition, the presence of an automatic garage door opener, and any potential safety hazards. Two obvious problems are found in garages. One is cracked cement, typically due to the cement settling at different rates

Figure 5.3—Window Styles

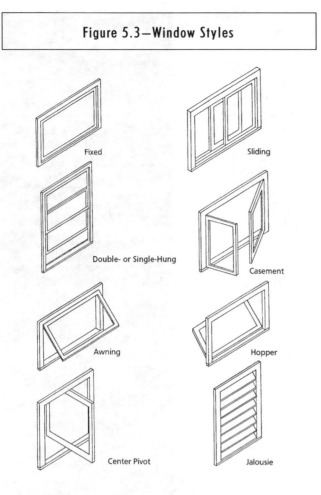

Fixed

Sliding

Double- or Single-Hung

Casement

Awning

Hopper

Center Pivot

Jalousie

Source: *Appraising Residential Properties,* 2d ed.
(Chicago: Appraisal Institute, 1994.)

(referred to as *differential settlement*) or the pressure of a high water table. A second problem is termite infestation at the point where the wood meets the ground. Less common problems include a buckling wall ((if the garage is below grade), oil stains and spills (a possible environmental consideration), and problems with the exterior siding and roof.

The primary item of functional obsolescence found in garages is an insufficient amount of car storage. Since more family members drive today, one-car garages are functionally obsolete in many areas of the country. Carports can also be functionally obsolete in markets where enclosed garages are the norm. On the other hand, in hot areas like Florida, carports are typical and the presence of a garage may be a superadequacy.

WOODEN DECKS
Wooden decks should be inspected for safety. If there are

INSPECTOR'S TIP

Problems can arise wherever wood touches the ground. The wood can rot or be affected by termites, carpenter ants, or powder post beetles. If termites are present, there will be shelter tubes or tunnels within the wood. The appraiser should obtain the permission of the owner and probe the wood with a screwdriver or pick to inspect for shelter tubes, galleries, or channels which run parallel to the grain inside the wood. Carpenter ants do not consume the wood like termites, but they can undermine its integrity by creating tunnels inside it. There will usually be small piles of sawdust around their excavations. Powder post beetles can be detected by looking for small holes on the outside of the wood where the larva have tunneled out; they tend to be found on the inside of homes and rarely on the outside. Because these insects undermine the integrity of the wood, a severe problem can result in a collapsed deck and possible injury. Wet and dry rot further undermine the structural capacity of wood.

obvious signs of deterioration, such as decaying boards, this represents a hazard that should be noted in the appraisal. Decay often occurs when the wood has not been pressure-treated to withstand water and moisture. Although few appraisers check for termites, they should know the telltale signs and mention the infestation in the report.

Other items to inspect include the joint that connects the deck to the home and the underlying support beams below the planking. If the joint connecting the deck to the home is corroded, the deck's structural integrity may be compromised. If the underlying support beams are rotted or cracked, there is a potential for deck collapse. Lastly, if there are few or no guardrails and the deck is elevated, this is a safety hazard for children. Many decks are not up to local building codes and the township may not allow the home to be sold until the problem is corrected.

INTERIOR INSPECTION

The inspection of the interior begins with the main entrance to the home. The appraiser should describe the construction and condition of the interior in sufficient detail to allow the reader of the appraisal to picture it mentally. All potential problems that may lead to major repair expenses should be identified. When walking through the home, the appraiser will note any apparent problems that should be discussed in the report. Cracks in the concrete may indicate settlement of the building or possibly a structural problem. Plasterboard walls may have popping nails which require cosmetic repair. Water stains and broken ceiling tiles should also be noted. Bulging walls indicate a moisture problem behind the wall and often coincide with cracks or other openings in the building exterior. Such problems should be prominently mentioned in the appraisal. The appraiser should check for a sufficient number of electrical outlets and notice how many are two-prong (not grounded) and three-prong (grounded).

INTERIOR FLOOR PLANS
Although it may seem simple, drawing an accurate interior floor plan is often one of the most difficult tasks encountered by novice residential appraisers. If the appraiser has used graph paper to draw the exterior to scale, the interior floor plan can be drawn to scale inside the exterior sketch.

It is impractical to measure the interior walls and distances when walking through the home. Household furnishings may be in the way and getting an accurate reading can disrupt family life. Fortunately, Fannie Mae guidelines do not require interior measurements. Only an approximate layout is needed to show the functional utility of the floor plan. With this in mind, an appraiser who knows the length of his or her stride can walk off the length of the walls and judge the distances between them. Sometimes the location of exterior features can provide an interior guide—e.g., an interior wall may be parallel to the edge of a porch or an exterior door.

As mentioned earlier, an electronic measuring device can be used for interior measurements. The appraiser can simply place the device adjacent to one wall and measure the distance to the opposite wall.

Descriptive Symbols

Appraisers have adopted a set of symbols to help identify the location of doors, windows, bathroom fixtures, closets, and other features to be included in the floor plan. Many of these symbols are also used in popular computer sketching programs. Figure 5.4 shows common symbols used to identify typical household features.

Floor Plan Example

Figure 5.5 is an example of a floor plan drawn in the field. A final version of the same floor plan produced by a sketching program is presented in Figure 5.6. Many experienced appraisers use abbreviations for interior components such as "F" for a fireplace and "C" for closets. Appropriate symbols are created by the sketching software.

CALCULATION OF GROSS LIVING AREA

Gross living area is defined as "the total area of finished and above-grade residential space."[3] It is the standard unit of measurement for residential property and is recognized by federal agencies involved with lending, including Fannie Mae, Freddie Mac, the FHA, and the VA.. Gross living area is calculated as follows:

1. Measure the length of all first-floor walls.
2. If the home has more than one level, determine the size of each above-grade floor.
3. Exclude the basement area, even if it is finished and heated. A finished basement should be considered either finished, below-grade area or finished basement area, not gross living area.
4. Exclude any garage, shed, carport, or other outbuilding that is not heated and fully finished.
5. Exclude all open and enclosed porches that are not finished and heated.
6. Exclude balconies and decks.

Figure 5.4—Common Home Interior Symbols

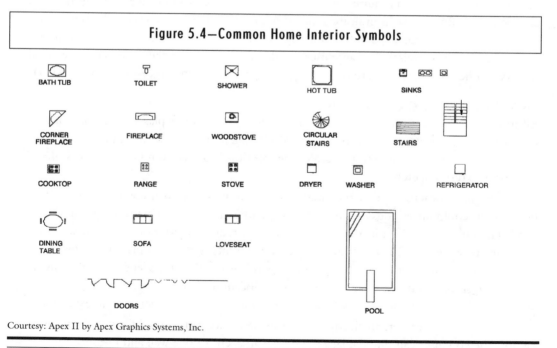

Courtesy: Apex II by Apex Graphics Systems, Inc.

---

3. Appraisal Institute, *The Dictionary of Real Estate Appraisal,* 3d ed. (Chicago: Appraisal Institute, 1993), 164.

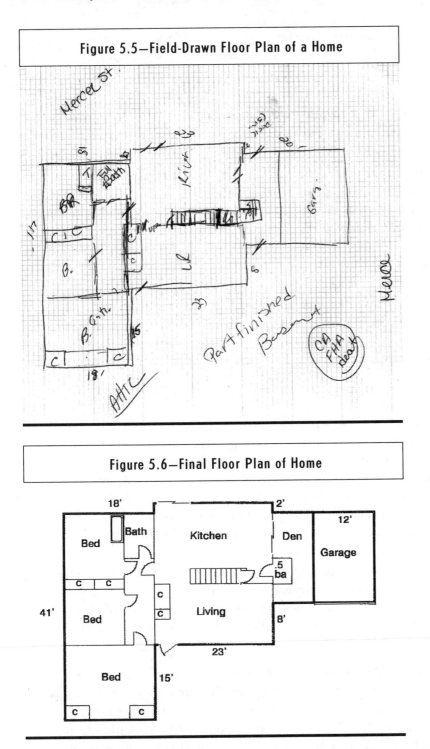

Figure 5.5—Field-Drawn Floor Plan of a Home

Figure 5.6—Final Floor Plan of Home

7. If the attic is finished, heated, and has at least a five-foot clear ceiling height, its area should be included. Any part of the attic that does not meet these criteria should not be included.

Difficulties in Calculating Gross Living Area

Sometimes appraisers have a difficult time calculating gross living area. Bi-level homes (also known as raised ranches) and split levels present problems when the lower level is heated and finished in a manner similar to the rest of the home. Partial upper stories and significant roof slopes will affect interior gross living area. Some guidelines for these situations are described below.

Split levels and bi-levels. Section 404.06 of Fannie Mae's *Property and Appraisal Analysis* guide states, "We consider a level to be below-grade if any portion of it is below grade—regardless of the quality of its 'finish' or the window area of a room. Therefore, a walk-out basement with finished rooms would not be included in the above-grade room count."

Sloping roofs. Because the slope of the roof can vary, there is no set rule for determining the gross living area of a multilevel home. If the above-grade floor is full-sized, i.e., similar to the first floor, and the roof slope is moderate, one rule-of-thumb is to add 80% of the ground floor area to the gross living area. If the slope is more severe, a lower percentage should be used at the appraiser's discretion. In these situations, it is wise for the appraiser to state in the report how gross living area was determined.

Partial floors. When the above-ground floors are partial floors, the appraiser should determine the gross living area by measuring from the ground floor. This is done by measuring the length of the first-floor walls that parallel those on the second floor. The appraiser should avoid the "percentage of ground floor area" method whereby the appraiser assigns a percentage of the first-floor area to account for the partial floors. This is imprecise and faulty appraisal practice. Many split-level homes have partial second floors which approximate 50% of the ground floor level.

FLOOR PLAN FUNCTIONAL OBSOLESCENCE

In a residential inspection, the functionality of the floor plan is often overlooked. It is easy to note the construction features and deficiencies of a home while overlooking the functionality of the floor plan. Some types of floor plans are functionally obsolete in theory, but are accepted by most buyers; others are glaringly obsolete. For instance, a two-bedroom home is functionally obsolete in many markets and mortgage underwriters will only accept the appraisal if the comparable sales contain two bedrooms. (Three-bedroom homes are not considered comparable.)

The appraiser should understand the market in question, recognize if a floor plan has items of functional obsolescence, and assess the impact of the obsolescence on the marketability and/or value of the home. Most floor plans reflecting functional obsolescence fall into a few general categories. Common items of obsolescence in floor plans are identified in Table 5.3.

KITCHENS

The kitchen is widely acknowledged to be one of the most important rooms in a home and it receives the most floor traffic. Its general appearance is the first thing a home buyer notices when entering the kitchen, followed by its spaciousness and built-in appliances.

The layout of a kitchen is planned around the three points of the work triangle: the cooking area, the sink and food preparation area, and the refrigerator. Common layouts include the U-shaped kitchen and the L-shaped kitchen. A U-shaped kitchen has the cabinets and counters along three walls. Generally the sink is at the base of the U and the refrigerator and cooking area are on opposite sides, facing one another. This layout is very efficient. Larger U-shaped kitchens may have islands in the middle that contain a sink or cooking area. An L-shaped kitchen has counters arranged along two sides, with the refrigerator at one end and the cooking area along the perpendicular side. Other kitchen layouts include the corridor

Table 5.3—Functionally Obsolete Items in Floor Plans

PROBLEM AREA	DESCRIPTION
Front door and entrance	Front door leads to another door, creating an enclosed foyer; access to key areas such as the kitchen, bathrooms, or bedrooms is less convenient as a result.
	Front door leads directly into the living room.
	No coat closet near door.
Bathrooms	There is an insufficient number of full bathrooms in relation to the number of bedrooms or their location is inconvenient. In most markets, there should be at least one bathroom in a three-bedroom home and two in a home with four or more bedrooms.
	Bedrooms are upstairs and the bath is downstairs.
Living room	Bedrooms or bathrooms are visible from the living room.
Kitchen	No door to outside from the kitchen or pantry.*
	Location and type of appliances do not meet market tastes.
	Kitchen eating area is too small.
	Bathroom is located directly off the kitchen.
	Kitchen is located in the front of the house.*
Stairways	Stairway is accessible through a bedroom, not a hallway.
Extensions/recreation room	Extensions do not connect with the kitchen or pantry.
Basements	No door to the outside.
	No powder room in a finished basement; occupants must walk up to the first floor to use a restroom.
Closets	Insufficient number or size of closets.
Ceiling height	Ceiling height is too low or too high.

* This item would not be regarded as functionally obsolete in all markets.

kitchen, which has cabinets on opposite sides with no adjoining section, and the strip kitchen, which has only one counter for all the appliances and the cooking area. Typical kitchen layouts are depicted in Figure 5.7.

Inspection

The following list highlights important items to be considered in a kitchen inspection.

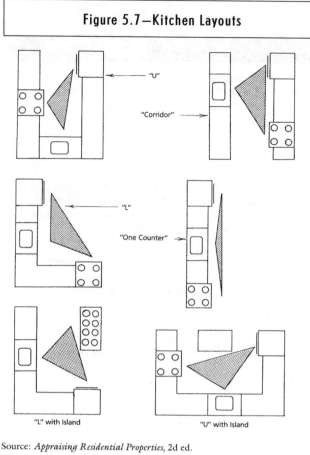

Figure 5.7—Kitchen Layouts

"U"

"Corridor"

"L"

"One Counter"

"L" with Island

"U" with Island

Source: *Appraising Residential Properties,* 2d ed.
(Chicago: Appraisal Institute, 1994), 201.

- How large is the kitchen? Is it sufficiently large for a typical home buyer in this market? Kitchen size will be proportional to the age, quality, and price of the home.

- Does the kitchen show significant signs of wear? Is it outdated?

- Is the kitchen adjacent to the dining room?

- Does the kitchen get natural sunlight through windows or skylights?

- Is there sufficient cabinet storage?

- Does the kitchen have a single or double basin?

- What appliances are built-in? These may include a dishwasher, trash compactor, microwave, garbage disposal, oven, range top, refrigerator, hot water heater, hood/fan, gas grill, and others.

- Is the sink close enough to the refrigerator? Is there a counter adjacent to the refrigerator? Does the kitchen have a functional work triangle?

- Is there a smoke detector in the kitchen or in an adjacent room?

- Is there a hood over the stove with ducts and a fan to remove smoke?

BATHROOMS

Bathroom tastes have changed significantly over the years. Many older homes that have not been modernized suffer from small bathrooms or too few of them. Older, three-bedroom homes usually have only one full bathroom. This reflects functional obsolescence compared to newer homes, but not when compared to older homes in the same market. For the most part, a home should have at least one full and one half bathroom. Two-story homes should have one bathroom on each floor. In some areas, a standard bathroom in lieu of a master bathroom can be an item of functional obsolescence. The appraiser must know local market preferences to discern if functional obsolescence is present.

The sizes of bathrooms vary with the price and style of the home. As a general rule, a full-size bathroom must be at least five feet by seven feet. The minimum size for a powder room is four feet by five feet. Ideally, a full-size bathroom should measure at least six feet by eight feet.

Inspection

The appraiser should observe the following items and note their construction and condition:

- Size of bathroom.

- Number and type of bathroom fixtures (e.g., one tub and shower, one sink, and one toilet).

- Type of flooring, such as ceramic or vinyl tile, and how well it is affixed to the floor.

- Admission of natural light through windows and skylights.

- Amount and type of interior lighting.

- Presence or absence of ventilation fans.

- Age of the fixtures and construction. If the house has not been modernized, sometimes it is possible to discern its age by lifting the lid of the commode and noting the date stamped into the ceramic.

- If the bathroom has a tub, the absence of a shower may or may not be an item of functional obsolescence, depending on the market.

- Grouting and condition of shower walls.

- Wall covering such as ceramic tile, wallpaper, or paint.

- How many bedrooms are there per bathroom? If the occupants of more than two bedrooms share a bathroom, this may reflect functional obsolescence in newer homes. In older homes, this is more common.

- Type of ceiling.

- Items of deterioration such as water stains on the ceilings or walls, standing water on the floor, wet rot, soft floors, discolored floor coverings, or grouting problems. The appraiser will want to check to see if there are cracks in the grout between the ceramic tiles around the tub. If any of the tiles are loose or will yield to pressure, the underlying wall may have been water damaged and should be repaired.

Newer homes will have a master bathroom off the master bedroom and a second full bath to accommodate the other second-floor bedrooms. At a minimum, a half bath should be located on the first floor.

LIVING ROOMS, FAMILY ROOMS, AND DENS

Living rooms and family rooms are the primary social areas in a home. The sizes of these rooms are important because the home may be functionally obsolete if they are too small to accommodate the family of a typical buyer.

One important item in living and family rooms is the type of floor covering. Some markets view hardwood floors as upscale and they add to a home's value as a result. In other markets good-quality carpeting, tile, marble, stone, or other floor coverings are preferred. The appraiser

INSPECTOR'S TIP

With the owner's permission, you can check the water pressure by turning on the tub and sink faucets and then flushing the toilet. The water pressure will drop somewhat, but if it declines significantly, this could indicate a problem that should be noted within the report.

INSPECTOR'S TIP

If the faucets are quickly turned on and then off, you may hear a loud rumbling noise and feel vibrations, known as *hammering*. It is generally not a problem, but it could damage the pipes. This can be corrected by installing an antiknock coil or air chamber.

should learn what types of floor coverings add to marketability and value in their region.

Other items sometimes found in living rooms or family rooms include skylights, fireplaces, and different types of ceilings. Newer homes may have vaulted or tray ceilings or a floor one step below grade. Skylights are usually seen in conjunction with vaulted ceilings. The appraiser should note if skylights are fixed in place or can be opened with either a hand crank or pole. If they can be opened, there is a greater chance of roof leaks, although the slope of the roof usually directs the water away.

The two most common functional problems in living rooms are too much traffic through the living room to get to other areas of the house and insufficient size or a layout that does not accommodate a comfortable arrangement of furniture.

BEDROOMS

Considered together, bedrooms comprise more floor area than any other part of a home. Two-story homes usually have all the bedrooms on the second floor, but some have the master bedroom on the first floor. According to FHA standards, a bedroom must contain at least one closet.

The most important things to note about bedrooms are their number, size, proximity to bathrooms, and the number of closets. In a newer home, the master bedroom should have a master bath. Many newer homes offer a variety of closet types and built-ins, including separate his and her walk-in closets. The appraiser should note the amount of closet storage available in each bedroom. The number of windows and the amount of sun or shade the bedrooms receive can also be important to a home's marketability.

DINING ROOMS

Dining rooms were once used nightly for family dinners, but today's busy families now use them mostly for entertaining guests. Older homes usually have separate dining rooms, but in newer homes the dining room is often open to the kitchen and sometimes to the kitchen and the living room or recreation room. If a dining room is not included in a home, a large, eat-in kitchen must be available.

Dining rooms frequently suffer functional obsolescence. Lighting can be poor, partitioning may be absent when the market demands it, or the space may be insufficient to accommodate a reasonable arrangement of the table and chairs. Stairs may open into the dining room or it may be awkwardly placed within the home, without convenient access to the kitchen.

FIREPLACES AND CHIMNEYS

Fireplaces are found in both new and older homes. Most home owners rarely use the fireplace but, like a whirlpool, this feature is demanded in the marketplace. Most new home projects offer one fireplace in a central gathering area such as the living room, with more fireplaces available as options.

Fireplaces vary substantially in design and effectiveness. Most have only one opening, although some contemporary homes feature a two-opening fireplace which can serve two rooms.

Inspection

The most common problems with fireplaces are insufficient draft protection, carpeting that is too near to the opening, inadequate size, inadequate hearth area to protect the room, and poor energy efficiency. The appraiser can usually determine if the fireplace has a draft by standing in front of it and reaching into the chimney. When there is a draft, cold air blows through the chimney and increases heating bills in the winter. The appraiser should also note if carpeting is placed too close to the fireplace opening where a stray spark could ignite it. Many newer fireplaces have glass doors that slide over the opening, preventing drafts and sparks from entering the room. The appraiser should also check:

- The exterior joints between the chimney and the wall. Cracks in the joints are usually not a problem because they most likely result from the natural settlement of the house. Nevertheless, they should be sealed to prevent moisture intrusion.

- The flashing that connects the roof to the chimney, which may show signs of wear.

- Any location where the chimney has cracked, missing, or loose sections of mortar. This potentially dangerous condition should be noted.

- The presence of rust on metal chimneys.

BASEMENTS

Interior Finishing

When inspecting a finished basement, the appraiser notes the size of the basement, the square footage of finished area, the quality of finish, the heating and cooling systems, the number of electrical outlets, the lighting, and the clear ceiling height. It is not uncommon for property record cards to omit finished basements, and the appraiser cannot rely on the assessor's determination of finish or square footage.

The quality of construction and type of interior finish is important. Many basements are finished with paneling, which is acceptable in older homes, but may not meet market demands in newer or larger homes. The basement finish is almost always of lower quality than the finish of above-grade floors. Ceiling height can be a problem because the basements of older homes were designed with much lower ceilings, which can be a form of functional obsolescence. The heating unit and ductwork should be examined because heating efficiency varies widely. The age of the heating unit can be determined by examining the date of construction on the heater's faceplate. The appraiser should also note whether a half or full bath is provided in the finished basement; if there is no bathroom, this is usually considered functional obsolescence. Finally, the basement's insulation and lighting should be noted. It is not uncommon to find relatively poor-quality lighting, low electrical amperage, and little or no insulation in a basement.

Potential Problems

Basements are often problem areas in homes and they can be costly to fix. Value and marketability can be greatly affected because home buyers equate the condition of the basement with the structural integrity of the home. If there is a problem, most home buyers will lose interest, regardless of how attractive the rest of the home is. The magnitude of one type of basement problem is reflected in the following statistic:

About 60 percent of all houses in this country suffer from some form of below ground wetness. Block foundations are especially vulnerable, with an 80 to 90 percent chance of leakage within the first 20 years.[4]

Most basement problems involve cracks and foundation settling or water and moisture accumulation.

Cracks and foundation settling. Cracks at ground level on the outside or along the inside walls of a basement are an obvious sign of trouble. These cracks cannot be concealed with paint for any length of time because of house settlement and the slight expansion and contraction that occurs as moisture levels and temperatures change.

Cracks can have many causes. When a new building settles evenly, this is called *uniform settlement.* The minor cracks that result are irregularly patterned or straight. As long as the basement is waterproofed, these cracks are rarely a problem for the home owner.

When a new building settles unevenly, however, differential settlement results. The most obvious sign of differential settlement is a stairlike cracking of concrete block walls, usually evident in the basement. This more severe problem is often aggravated over time because sections of the building are settling at different rates. Serious differential settlement problems can undermine the structural integrity of a house. Walls and ceilings can become cracked, floors can become uneven, and moisture problems increase.

Differential settlement occurs in all homes. It is usually a problem when the soil has not compacted sufficiently from the weight of the home. Older homes do not generally have this problem because the settlement has occurred long ago.

Although the appraiser is not required to be a home inspector, it is appropriate to note the presence of basement cracks and briefly discuss them in the report.

Water and moisture accumulation. A damp or musty smell is the first sign that a basement has, or has had, moisture problems. Wetness can come from interior condensation and leaks or from exterior drainage into the basement through wall and floor cracks. A problem can occur quickly (e.g., a pipe bursting) or develop slowly. Most leaks are caused by the accumulation of water outside the house due to poor drainage. In newer homes, the problem is usually poorly designed grading outside the home, a poor selection of moisture-barrier materials, or insufficient basement waterproofing. Condensation usually occurs when warm air comes in contact with a cold water pipe.

The municipal engineer may know if an area has a high water table, which may cause basement problems. It is unlikely, however, that the engineer would know about basement leaks in individual homes.

---

4. American Society of Home Inspectors, "Wet Basements and Crawl Spaces" brochure.

The appraiser should look for the following signs, which may indicate a moisture problem:

- A damp, musty smell. At the very least, the odor should be noted in the report along with any obvious signs of water damage.
- Wooden beams that show sign of rot. The appraiser can examine the wood beams that support the ground floor (the ceiling of the basement) and use a pick, screwdriver, or pocket knife to probe the wood, with the owner's consent.
- Water spots on carpets, walls, paneling, or ceiling tiles.
- Signs of mildew on carpets or walls.
- Mold, fungi, yeast, or plants growing in wall cracks.
- Water accumulation on the floor.
- Rust on the legs of heating equipment or steel beam columns.
- Peeling paint on the walls.
- Efflorescence, a white, powdery salt that comes from the masonry wall and is deposited as it dries. The appraiser should look along the lower section of the foundation walls or at the joint where the wall meets the slab floor.
- Bulging interior finishes such as paneling or sheetrock.
- If the floor covering is tile, areas of deterioration, loose tiles, or efflorescence between the tile cracks.
- Condensation on one or more pipes.

ATTICS

Many appraisers fail to inspect the attic, especially during the summer when it is uncomfortable to do so. This is problematic because most home buyers do not look at attics critically, if at all. The market rarely ascribes value and marketability differences to attics. If something is wrong with the attic, however, and the appraiser failed to inspect it, potential liability exists.

The most important attic characteristics for an appraiser to consider are air flow, insulation, and roof leakage. Air flow is enhanced by ridge vents at the peak of the roof, electric or wind-powered vents along the sides of the attic, or turbines installed on the roof. Soffits, which are metal vents underneath the roof overhang, should also be present and can be viewed from the outside. Sufficient insulation should also be in place, although it can be difficult to ascertain how much has been installed if wooden boards lie over the rafters.

When attics are finished, they should be inspected like any other room in the house. Since the quality of attic finish and workmanship is usually not the same as the rest of the home, the appraiser should note how functional the space appears to be. Particular attention should be paid to flooring, lighting, access, finish, quality, size, electrical and heating outlets, and the amount of clear ceiling height.

Inspection

When inspecting an attic, the appraiser should be aware of safety and energy efficiency. If the attic has no finished floor, the appraiser should be careful to step on the rafters; stepping between the rafters is unsafe and the appraiser could unintentionally penetrate the ceiling of the room below. Insulation should be installed between the rafters on the floor, not attached to the underside of the roof. Ventilation stacks from below that terminate in the attic are a potential fire hazard and usually a violation of the plumbing code. The stack should extend through the attic to the outside. Water stains or other evidence of leakage on the roof rafters or planks indicates a previous or current problem.

INSULATION

In the inspection of insulation, appraisers are again concerned with safety and energy efficiency. If the subject is an older home, the appraiser should ask the property owner about the type of insulation present. The concern here is the presence of asbestos insulation. Of course, many owners who know asbestos is present will not disclose this information.

The second consideration is energy efficiency. An R factor is an indication of the insulation's resistance to heat transfer. An R factor of one is equivalent to the heat resistance of one inch of wood. Many homes have floor and wall insulation with an R factor of 19 and 30 R insulation for the ceiling. Single-pane windows have an R factor of about 0.5, which is why most temperature transfer occurs through windows, not walls. Although a home may be designed with insulation with an R factor of 19, over the course of many years the R factor declines. For this reason, the appraiser should get into the habit of asking the owner when the walls, ceilings, and attic were last insulated and the R factor of the insulation used.

Asbestos

Asbestos is a concern for both commercial and residential property owners. Asbestos is a natural fibrous mineral which does not burn, has high tensile strength, cannot be corroded, and provides excellent insulation. Unfortunately, it has been proven to cause cancer with sufficient exposure under certain conditions.

Asbestos is no longer used for residential and commercial construction, but it was very prevalent from 1930 to 1978. It is found in many common construction materials such as vinyl floor tiles, ceiling tiles, roof shingles, paints, ductwork connections, boiler and pipe insulation, and wall and attic insulation. Problems with asbestos are very expensive to correct because asbestos crumbles, creates airborne fibers, and is difficult to dispose of. Owners of older commercial properties with asbestos often will not try to remove it, choosing ongoing mitigation instead.

Asbestos in a building does not automatically result in a problem. Unless the asbestos becomes friable (i.e., easy to crumble with the potential to become airborne), an ongoing maintenance program can keep a building safe. If it is not friable, the asbestos should not be disturbed. The specific details of the asbestos mitigation program should be described in the appraisal report.

Inspection. There are many areas in which asbestos can be found.

- In a home or small commercial property, it is common to find old boilers which have been insulated with asbestos. The appraiser should look for a white coating material on the outside of the water heater similar to a heater jacket.

- Asbestos may have been sprayed as insulation behind the walls. However, there is virtually no way to determine this unless the owner provides the information or there are holes in the wall which the appraiser can inspect. Sometimes removal of an electrical socket can provide access and allow the appraiser to determine if asbestos fibers are present.

- Another common area for asbestos insulation is around the heating pipes in the basements or crawl spaces of older homes. Viewed from the edge of the insulating sheet, the asbestos will look like corrugated cardboard. Fittings around the angled portion of the pipes may have a plaster-like insulation which is also made of asbestos.

- Removing one or more acoustic tile panels from a ceiling and inspecting above the remaining tiles may reveal loose asbestos fibers. Of course, permission should be obtained from the owner before the tiles are removed.

- Asbestos sheet insulation may be found in the attic.

ELECTRICAL SYSTEMS

The electrical system should not be overlooked in the inspection. Many appraisers do not realize that inadequate wiring can be dangerous and an item of functional obsolescence. On the other hand, appraisers are not home inspectors and cannot be held accountable for determining electrical adequacy. The electrical capacity of a home can be very difficult to pinpoint.

Determining Electrical Capacity

There are two ways to determine the electrical capacity in a home. To determine voltage, the appraiser can examine the service drop, i.e., the overhead wires that run from the telephone poles to the roof of the house. These wires are attached to the home by a metal pipe called a service entrance. By counting the number of wires affixed to the service entrance, the appraiser can get a good indication of the electrical power available to the home. If there are two wires, which is typical of older homes, a 110 or 120 volt service is indicated; three wires, which are common in more modern homes, indicate 120 and 240 volt service. Typically, a 110 or 120 volt service will indicate 30- to 60-amp electrical

APPRAISER'S TIP

To determine amperage, the appraiser can examine the power cable that runs into the circuit breaker box. The thickness of the wire running into the main circuit box determines its amperage. For instance, a 200-amp wire is much thicker than a 100-amp wire. It is important that the appraiser be able to assess the thickness of this wire visually and determine its corresponding amperage.

INSPECTOR'S TIP

A good way to determine if there is a problem with the electrical current in a house is to use a voltage detector. This hand-held device costs $20 to $100 and can detect electromagnetic current. It can be used around almost any metal surface to verify the proper electrical grounding of the fuse box and the adequacy of wiring or switches. Simply point the device at the suspect item and, if the alarm goes off, it is likely that excess current is being funneled through it. If an electrical panel is "hot" and someone touches the metal, the resulting shock can be fatal. Needless to say, this device can be a life saver as well as reducing business risk.

service in the home, which is inadequate for all but the smallest homes. The electrical service may have been upgraded and the appraiser should get in the habit of questioning the owner on this point whenever possible. If the home is newer and there are no overhead wires, the electrical service is underground. There is a very good chance that the underground electrical service is 240 volt; the building department should be able to verify this fact.

Common mistakes. Many appraisers make the mistake of looking at the label in the circuit breaker panel to check the amperage and voltage of the system. They then add up the amperage of the individual circuits to determine total amperage. This is incorrect because the amperage figure on the inside of the circuit breaker panel represents the amperage of the box, not the wires. The sum of the amperage of the circuits inside is greater than the amperage of the box because not all electrical outlets will be used simultaneously at their maximum capacity. The highest amperage of the main circuit breaker determines amperage capacity.

Another common misperception is that the total amperage of the home equals the sum of the amperages on each of the circuit breaker boxes, not the amperage of the individual circuits themselves. This is incorrect because the individual circuit breaker boxes draw power from the main breaker box, and the number of amps on the main circuit breaker box determines the power rating for the entire home. For example, if the main circuit breaker box in a newly built home has 200 amps of power and there are two 60-amp circuit boxes, the total amperage is not 200 + 60 + 60, or 320; it is 200 because the secondary 60-amp boxes draw power from the original 200-amp main breaker.

Electrical System Functional Obsolescence

Over the past few decades, residents have added many new types of appliances to make their homes more convenient. Both electrical capacity and conductive materials have changed. Inadequate electrical service is the primary cause of home electrical fires.

Most older homes were designed with 60-amp capacity, which is inadequate for today's needs. Major appliances such as air-conditioning systems, heat pumps, clothes dryers, and stoves require 150 to 240 amps of power. Obviously, a 60-amp system is inadequate for these uses and could result in power overloads and even fires. Systems with 100 amps are better, but they still may be inadequate in some market areas.

In general, a substantial number of homes 20 or more years old have an inadequate power supply. Appraisers may disagree about how much electrical capacity constitutes functional obsolescence; this depends on market perceptions. However, most would agree that a 60-amp system is functionally obsolete; some believe anything less than 100 amps and 120/240 volt service is obsolete. Table 5.4 can be used as a guide to determine the adequacy of a home's electrical capacity.

Although the electrical service in a home may be inadequate for large, power-hungry appliances, it may be just fine for small families with less intensive needs. To determine if the electrical capacity is adequate, the appraiser must first assess the needs of the typical home buyer in the neighborhood and then compare them to the electrical capacity of the home. If the system is judged to be inadequate, it may be necessary to apply an adjustment for the electrical system's functional obsolescence in the report. Table 5.5 outlines the power requirements of many major appliances.

One noteworthy trend is the increased prevalence of home offices. Home offices can tax a home's electrical capacity because some older computer systems and office machines use a tremendous amount of power. However, the advent of computer components that draw less electricity has reduced the need for more electrical capacity to power home office equipment. Still, in homes with less than 200 amps of power, lights will usually dim when power-intensive equipment is operating. Because home computers and peripheral computer components are increasingly popular, homes may soon include more amperage as part of their design.

Another type of functional obsolescence involves the conductors used to transfer electricity. Some homes constructed from the 1950s through the 1970s contained aluminum wiring. Unfortunately, aluminum wiring can oxidize over time, which results in higher electrical resistance. Higher electrical resistance can cause power overloads, overheating of wires, and fires. When these problems were first discovered, many municipalities quickly passed laws prohibiting aluminum wiring in homes.

Table 5.4—Adequacy of Electrical Service			
AMPERAGE	VOLTAGE	WATTAGE	ADEQUACY RATING
30	110	3,300	Inadequate
30	110/220	6,600	Inadequate
60	110	6,600	Inadequate
60	110/220	13,200	Marginal for a small house without major appliances
100	110/220	22,000	Minimum
150	110/220	33,000	Good
200	110/220	44,000	Very good

Source: Norman Becker, *The Complete Book of Home Inspection* (New York: TAB Books, 1993), 139.

Table 5.5—Power Requirements of Appliances	
APPLIANCE	POWER REQUIREMENT IN WATTS
Attic fan	400
Central air-conditioning	6,000
Clothes dryer	4,500
Dishwasher	1,500
Forced-air electric furnace	28,000
Freezer	575
Garbage disposal	900
Hand iron	1,000
Instant hot water dispenser	1,000
Lamp (each bulb)	25-150
Microwave oven	500
Electric range	8,000
Portable room heater	1,600
Room air conditioner	1,100
Sauna	8,000
Steam bath generator	7,500
Color television	150-450
Water heater	2,500-4,500

Source: Norman Becker, *The Complete Book of Home Inspection*
(New York: TAB Books, 1993), 139

Signs of electrical inadequacy. There are five primary indications that a home's electrical system is inadequate.

1. An inordinate number of extension cords are in use throughout the home. Extension cords have a lower electrical capacity than the outlet itself.

2. Circuit breakers trip or fuses blow frequently.

3. Smoke is emitted from receptacles which have heavy power drains.

4. When a major appliance is in use, the picture on the television set is affected.

5. Lights dim or flicker when appliances are activated.

PLUMBING

Determining the adequacy and potential functional obsolescence of plumbing is difficult. The plumbing may be inadequate, but if a typical buyer would not notice the deficiency, functional obsolescence would not be reflected in the home's sale price. Most appraisers confine their inspection to simply asking the home owner about the condition of the plumbing, turning on the faucets to see if there is sufficient water pressure, determining if there are any leaks, and examining the plumbing fixtures. The house's piping may be made of copper, iron, lead, or polyvinyl chloride (PVC). Copper is usually considered superior; PVC pipes do not meet plumbing codes in some areas.

One plumbing item that is easily checked is the water heater. Most older homes have 40-gallon water heaters, which are adequate for small- to medium-sized homes. Although 40-gallon water heaters are installed in some newer homes today, many builders install heaters of 50 gallons or more in larger homes. Since larger homes accommodate more residents, it follows that a larger water heater would be needed. The appraiser will need to determine what size water heater is demanded by the market; one that is too large or too small may be an item of functional obsolescence.

Inspection

When inspecting a home's plumbing, the appraiser is limited to visible items such as the fixtures and basement plumbing. The appraiser will want to check the piping material used and its condition as well as the adequacy of the water pressure.

It can be difficult to determine if metal pipes are iron or copper. The pipes may be painted or soiled and their appearance can be deceiving. The simplest way to determine the pipe material is to use a magnet. If the magnet is attracted, the pipes are iron; otherwise, they are copper. Sometimes a home has mixed plumbing. Various sections may be made of iron, plastic, copper, or some combination of these materials. This is not good because iron and copper react to one another and corrosion is accelerated in a process called *galvanic corrosion*. Where iron and copper pipes meet, white mineral deposits form on the outside of the pipes. This problem will need correcting.

Any signs of mineral deposits or leakage on or near the plumbing system could indicate a problem that should be noted. Sometimes brass piping can have pinhole leaks. These form when the zinc inside the brass pipes dissolves, allowing water to leak and white mineral deposits to form.

As mentioned earlier, water pressure may be reduced when several plumbing fixtures are

INSPECTOR'S TIP

When a whirlpool is present in a home, the appraiser should pay special attention to the size of the water heater. A 40- or 50-gallon water heater cannot provide hot water to a whirlpool and satisfy all the household's other hot water needs. Some developers offer a larger water heater as an option or provide an additional water heater to supply the whirlpool.

INSPECTOR'S TIP

The inlet service pipe is a common problem area for older homes. This pipe has a meter on it and is usually found in the basement or on the foundation. If the pipe is made of lead, it could be depositing significant quantities of lead into the water. (Lead inlet water pipes have a bulge near the shutoff valve, a visual clue that it is indeed a lead pipe). The water should be tested to determine if this is the case.

operated at once. A slight reduction is typical, but greatly reduced pressure probably indicates a problem. Sometimes there is no problem with the plumbing in the house and the low water pressure is due to constriction of the main water pipe delivering water to the home. The low water pressure should be noted in the appraisal report.

HEATING AND AIR-CONDITIONING

There are many types of heating and cooling systems, including a forced-air furnace, hot water and steam, heat pump, baseboard radiant heating, wall-mounted heating or air-conditioning units, space heaters, and solar heating and cooling. The systems may use gas, electricity, oil, propane, wood, or other fuels. The degree of functional obsolescence present depends on the market's perception of the operating efficiency of the system, its safety, and the cost of alternative fuels.

Some types of systems work well in one area, but poorly in others. Heat pumps are common and accepted in moderate climates in the South, but they are inefficient and often functionally obsolete in colder areas. The appraiser should know what systems are accepted in his or her region.

Beyond identifying the systems and making sure they work properly, appraisers do not have extensive liability in this area. Heating and air-conditioning systems are expensive to fix or replace, so, if possible, the appraiser should turn on both systems to ensure that they are operational. The appraiser should check to make sure the fan is running, determine that hot or cool air comes through the vents when the system is turned on, and check the vents. If possible, the efficiency rating of the system and its age should be noted. Lastly, a limiting condition should be included in the report stating that an extensive examination of the systems was not undertaken and that an HVAC contractor should be contacted for a further investigation.

Inspection of Heating Systems

Like the plumbing system, a heating system can only be inspected to a limited extent. When the appraiser arrives for the inspection, he or she should verify that the heating system is operational. Activating the system out of season is not advised because the system could be damaged. If the system is not turned on, however, a disclaimer should accompany the appraisal report.

To determine if the home is heated by steam, hot water, or warm air, the appraiser should look at the heating unit and the type of heating outlets. Boilers should be examined for rust, mineral deposits, and evidence of leaks. The appraiser can determine if the return ducts for the heating system are working properly by placing a piece of paper over the vent. If it adheres to the vent, the return duct is working properly. Visible distribution pipes and areas below radiators should also be examined for signs of leaks.

Gravity warm-air heating systems are outdated and may be regarded as functionally obsolete, depending on local market preferences. A gravity system is not energy efficient. Such systems are prevalent in older homes, but are not used in newer construction. A gravity warm-air heating system can be converted to a forced hot water system.

If the heating system is fueled by oil, the appraiser should ask the home owner for the date of its last inspection. Over time, an oil burner can loose much of its efficiency and periodic inspection is necessary to keep the system operating at its peak. There is often a card or tag attached to the unit which describes its service history.

Inspection of Air-Conditioning Systems

If the outside temperature is below 60 degrees, turning on the air-conditioning system may damage it. Instead, the appraiser can assume it is operational and include a disclaimer in the report. The cooling capacity of an air-conditioning system is measured in British thermal units (BTUs). One BTU is equal to the amount of heat required to raise the temperature of a pound of water by one degree. The appraiser should check the faceplate on the air-conditioning compressor. The model number will indicate the capacity in code, or the full load amperage or rated load amperage will be noted. Table 5.6 indicates the encoded air-conditioning capacities of units made by major manufacturers. Dividing the full load amperage or the rated load amperage figure on the faceplace by 7 provides an approximate indication of the system's cooling capacity in tons.

If an air-conditioning system is too large, it will not work efficiently. It will cool the home quickly, but not be on long enough to remove moisture from the air. If the system is too small, it may operate almost all the time but not provide enough cooling to make the home comfortable. As a general rule-of-thumb, every 550 square feet of gross building area should have one ton of air-conditioning, or 12,000 BTUs.

Heat pumps are common in mild climates, but not in cold weather areas. A heat pump cannot supply sufficient heat in freezing temperatures. It is common to find backup heating components to augment the lower capacity of heat pumps during cold winter days. This type of system is very good for air-conditioning homes, but may be functionally obsolete for heating homes in cold climates.

OTHER POTENTIAL PROBLEMS

Three additional potential problems are worth noting: radon, lead, and electromagnetic radiation. All three can present health hazards and market perceptions will determine their effect on value and marketability.

Radon

Radon is an odorless, colorless gas that is naturally produced from radioactive deposits in the ground. Prolonged exposure to high levels of radon can cause cancer. The gas can travel up from the ground through cracks in basement floors and walls, cracks in concrete block walls, sump pits, and other openings in the building. Purchasers of property who are concerned about radon can have a test performed to determine if the gas is present. A canister is left on

Table 5.6—Capacity of Air-Conditioning Systems

MANUFACTURER	MODEL #	BTUs/HOUR	TONS
General Electric	BTB390A	30,000	2.5
Bryant	567CO36RCU	26,000	3
Carrier	38CC042-1	42,000	3.5
Tappan	CM48-42C	48,000	4

Source: Norman Becker, *The Complete Book of Home Inspection* (New York: TAB Books, 1993), 219

the premises for up to a week and the level of radon detected is measured. Radon testing is not routinely requested, so every appraisal should have a limiting condition about radon.

Lead

Lead poisoning is an insidious problem. Low doses can lead to hyperactivity and mental disorders; high doses can cause permanent brain injury or death. Children can get lead poisoning from ingesting peeling lead paint chips; other home occupants may suffer from extended exposure to lead dust in the air. Lead particles that settle on rugs or furniture can be picked up on hands and transmitted into the body through the mouth. The EPA has estimated that two-thirds of the homes constructed between 1940 and 1960 contain significant quantities of lead; even homes built up to the early 1980s have lead, although to a lesser degree.

There is no way to check if a home has large quantities of lead without conducting extensive scientific tests. Appraisers are not responsible for lead testing. The Department of Housing and Urban Development is now pioneering a certified lead abasement training program to mitigate the problem. Naturally, the appraiser should include a disclaimer in the assumptions and limiting conditions section of the appraisal report. If peeling paint is observed in an older home, there is a good chance that a lead problem exists. In this case the report should contain a limiting condition and describe the extent of the lead inspection undertaken in the description of the improvements and summary of salient facts.

Electromagnetic Radiation

We are all surrounded by electromagnetic radiation. Fortunately, very little of it is harmful. Two types of electromagnetic radiation can pose a hazard: magnetic fields and electrical fields. Both types of radiation are present in anything that uses electricity, such as transformers, electrical lines, wiring, and appliances. Of the two, magnetic fields are more serious because they can travel through most objects and walls without diminishing in intensity. Electrical fields can be blocked by various types of building materials and are generally not a major concern.

Members of the scientific community do not agree about the effects of electromagnetic fields. Some studies have suggested that they can increase birth defects in animals that receive prolonged exposure; other studies have linked electromagnetic fields to cancer. Whatever the validity of these studies, the public is very concerned about electromagnetic radiation. As a result, property values are usually lower for homes near high-tension power lines and marketing times tend to be much longer, even at lower prices.

Electromagnetic testing is not widely available. Government standards for electromagnetic radiation have not been formalized and no industry has been developed to measure it. As a result, it is highly unlikely that the appraiser will incur any liability in this regard. Nevertheless, it is wise to include a limiting condition in the report, especially if the subject is close to a high-tension power line, and to state that no testing was performed in the site description and summary of salient facts. The appraiser should apply an external obsolescence adjustment within the valuation sections of the report if the source of the electromagnetic radiation is close enough to be recognized by the market.

SUMMARY

Inspecting a home requires close observation of a great many items. Careful examination of the walls, roof, windows, deck, and other exterior elements can reveal a great deal about maintenance levels and suggest potential problems on the inside. When inspecting the interior, the appraiser has to look for the smallest details and still see the big picture. Home owners can be experts at disguising defects, so the appraiser must exercise due diligence by looking for and reporting all potential problems. Appraisers should be aware of the costs to cure various physical problems and consider the consequences of deferring repairs.

Many factors can create functional obsolescence in a building. It is very important to understand that the determination of functional obsolescence depends on market forces. An item that is not considered functionally obsolete in one market may have a major negative impact on value in another. In some instances, there may be no effect on value, but the marketing time for the property may be increased. It is the appraiser's job to determine if functional obsolescence is present and, if so, to determine its impact on value and marketability in the market in question.

CHAPTER 6

COMMERCIAL PROPERTY INSPECTION

Most appraisers learn the skills and techniques of commercial property inspection on the job. Although there are books on commercial building construction, little is available on commercial inspection procedures. Many of the items mentioned in regard to residential inspection in Chapter 5 also apply to commercial property inspections.

Large commercial properties usually have very complicated designs and systems, which require specialized knowledge. The inspection of commercial elevators, HVAC equipment, and plumbing systems is often beyond the appraiser's expertise. When large commercial properties are to be valued, engineering firms usually are retained to inspect the subject prior to its sale, thereby reducing the appraiser's liability.

GENERAL CONSIDERATIONS

Similar inspection procedures can be applied to residential and commercial properties because many of the building components are similar. For example, the plumbing, electrical, heating, and air-conditioning systems of a commercial property must be examined and the condition of the exterior, interior, roof, and site must be noted. However, a different emphasis may be placed on some inspection items since commercial properties are used and designed differently. Considerations such as handicapped access requirements and the adequacy of elevator and sprinkler systems are unique to commercial properties. More items of functional obsolescence are present in commercial buildings and market factors relating to the trade area, the environment, and local politics can be more significant.

AMERICANS WITH DISABILITIES ACT

On July 26, 1990, the Americans with Disabilities Act (ADA) became law. The importance of this act is emphasized below.

> The Act requires that all buildings used by public entities and places of public accommodations must now be accessible to disabled persons. Most building owners are not yet in compliance, and this creates a liability issue for both owners and mortgage lenders. As lenders become more aware of their potential liability in this area, they are beginning to require ADA compliance upon transfer of ownership or before refinancing.[1]

Appraisers have an obligation to state whether a property is required to conform to this act and to investigate whether or not it does. Fortunately, many items of conformance are easily observed. The property may have one or more parking spaces that are larger and identified with a handicapped symbol or sign. A concrete or wood ramp that leads to the front door may be provided along with an automatic door sensor and opening device. Restrooms should be larger to accommodate the turning radius of a wheelchair and doors must be wider to permit entry. A handbar near the toilet, a lower sink, and a low-height water fountain all indicate ADA compliance. A public pay phone with volume control and the presence of an elevator also contribute to accessibility for the disabled. Other items may be present depending on local codes, but if these obvious items are not found, it is unlikely that other items of conformance have been provided.

The appraiser should note the accommodations made and state whether the building appears to be in compliance. A limiting condition should be included in the report describing the extent of the appraiser's knowledge and the inspection procedure. Commercial appraisers are not expected to know every local code for handicapped access, but they are required to mention the obvious items of ADA conformance. It is also important to know when properties are exempt from ADA, e.g., historic properties. Exemptions may vary among municipalities.

INSPECTION OF BUILDING SYSTEMS

Electrical System

Electrical usage can be very difficult to pinpoint in commercial properties. Tenants may have different electrical needs, and sections of a building constructed at different times may have different power capabilities. The appraiser cannot simply look at the width of the wire leading into the circuit box to determine the number of amps in the building. The usage at the circuit box may be less than the total power coming into the building. All of these factors make it difficult to assess the electrical system in a commercial property.

There are various ways to determine an electrical system's capacity. Obviously, the owner should be asked how many amps come into the building and how many are distributed through the circuit boxes. The assessor, the building department, and the local power company can be contacted for information. If the building is leased, the electrical capacity

---

1. Dwayne De Vries and Alexander Meisel, "Assessment for Disabled Access Surveys: New Opportunities for Home Inspectors," *The ASHI Reporter* (September 1995), 14 and 15.

may be listed in one or more leases or on the tenant work letter. Lastly, the power available may be listed on one or more of the circuit boxes, although the amount shown may be less than that available at the transformer.

Because the demand for electrical power has increased, primarily due to the use of computer systems and specialized equipment, some older buildings have functionally obsolete electrical systems. A "smart" energy management system can allocate power among the various tenants to minimize shortages.

Heating and Air-Conditioning Systems

Examining the heating and air-conditioning systems in a commercial property can be problematic. Ducts are seldom accessible and therefore difficult to inspect. It is usually not practical to turn each system on and off to observe its operation. If one of the systems is operating during the inspection, its working order can be observed first-hand. Alternatively, the appraiser should find out if there is a service contract in place for the air-conditioning and heating units; if so, the servicing company can be a prime source of information. As a general rule, 125,000 BTUs of heat are needed for every 1,500 square feet of office area. Commercial appraisers often must question the owner, the manager, tenants, the service contract company, or municipal construction officials about the systems. The appraiser should plainly state in the report who was spoken to and the results of the conversation.

The appraiser should investigate potential problems with the HVAC system. The system may be poorly installed, provide insufficient air movement, or not be balanced properly. If the temperature on the southern side of a building increases due to the effects of the sun, more than one HVAC system may be required to compensate. System problems can result in higher utility expenses and repair costs. The appraiser should routinely ask if an HVAC analysis will be undertaken.

Sprinkler System

Sprinkler systems are easy to notice, but they cannot be turned on for obvious reasons. The appraiser should observe the number of sprinkler heads, the area covered by the sprinklers, and whether the system is wet or dry. The presence or absence of a service contract should also be noted. As a general rule, there should be one sprinkler head for every 100 square feet of area to be protected. Building codes concerning sprinklers will vary from one municipality to another and among various property types.

Plumbing System

The adequacy of plumbing systems can be difficult to assess. Turning on faucets and flushing toilets will not have any effect in most commercial properties because these systems are designed to handle high water and sewerage capacity. The appraiser will have to rely on information sources such as the owner, the tenants, and the water and sewer departments.

Roof

The majority of commercial properties have flat roofs, which are easy to inspect. The condition of the roof should always be observed and the presence or absence of a service contract should be noted. Many roofing companies guarantee their work for a certain number of years and the appraiser should inquire if a guarantee is in place. The inspection items discussed in the previous chapter also apply to the inspection of roofs on commercial properties. The appraiser should ask for a maintenance history to help determine if the building has a history of roof problems.

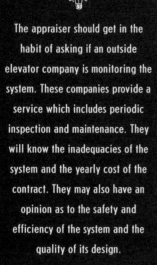
Elevators

Few appraisers have an in-depth knowledge of elevator systems and they are not expected to be experts in this area. The elevator should be in working order, meet the needs of building tenants, and provide satisfactory transportation for handicapped persons.

There are two types of elevator systems: electric and hydraulic. Electric elevators are found in buildings of all heights, but they are most prevalent in buildings of more than four stories. They are fast and usually computer-controlled. Hydraulic elevators are designed for low-rise buildings. They are simple to operate and much less expensive to maintain, but they are also slower and less responsive than electric systems.

Functional obsolescence found in elevators includes an insufficient number of cars (evidenced by long waiting times), no elevator service to below-grade parking levels, and a lack of a freight service for the entire height of the building. Freight elevators are needed to move furniture, goods, and refuse between upper floors and ground level.

INSPECTING SPECIFIC PROPERTY TYPES

VACANT LAND

Vacant land carries a high degree of business risk and a wide range of investigations are required to determine its development potential. Appraisers must offer opinions as to the amount of wetlands present on the subject and comparable sites, the impact of flood zone classifications, the soil's suitability for building, and the impact of nearby power lines. By rights, the only person fully qualified to make such determinations is an engineer. Although commercial appraisers are not expected to be engineers, they do need a working knowledge of a wide range of fields, especially land development. For this reason, it takes commercial appraisers many years to become proficient.

An accurate vacant land valuation begins with the site inspection procedures described in Chapter 4. A proper inspection will lay the foundation for a credible highest and best use analysis, comparable sales investigation, market analysis, and value conclusion.

PROPOSED RESIDENTIAL SUBDIVISIONS

The appraisal of a proposed residential subdivision can be very challenging. The approval and development process is long and complicated and appraisers must evaluate the current state of all approvals, development studies, and construction at the site. Although appraisers need not know all the nuances of the approval process, they should question the local planning board about the proposed subdivision's status in the approval process. Usually the board will use a checklist to organize the many mailings and correspondences necessary to monitor the subdivision and the appraiser can ask to see the checklist.

Another important item to request is a copy of the preliminary or final approval resolution. This document details what is needed for the approvals to be valid. Sometimes the approvals necessitate that an existing home on the site be demolished to make way for other homes. If the appraiser does not notice this, he or she may inadvertently include the home's value in the appraisal. The appraiser should inquire as to which conditions have been met and which remain. Then the developer can be consulted to see how the work is progressing. Estimating time of completion is important and the appraiser must often compare the developer's opinion with market-derived information.

Particular attention should be paid to the status of wetlands delineation, which can significantly affect the development time frame, the feasibility of the project, the development yield, and the value conclusion.

Subdivision appraisals are unique in that appraisers are commonly called upon to value developments that have approvals, but no formal development plans as yet. Often a project has only preliminary approvals, and the appraiser is asked to value the site as if approvals are in place based on a conceptual plan. The appraiser should be extremely careful when accepting such assignments because they call for a hypothetical, future value estimate that is subject to change. The well-defined reporting regulations set forth in the Uniform Standards of Professional Appraisal Practice must be strictly followed when hypothetical valuations are conducted. Problems are also encountered when an appraiser is required to estimate a value upon completion. This is often not a reasonable assumption because units will be sold off individually or in bulk before completion. Developers do not wait until the entire project is built to sell the units. The date of project completion must be estimated and clearly disclosed each time the value is reported. The importance of properly clarifying hypothetical valuations cannot be overemphasized.

> Caution should be exercised in such assignments because hypothetical value estimates can be misleading and inappropriate if the value is not properly identified. Hypothetical valuations should generally be avoided unless there is strong market support for the client's assumption."[2]

APPRAISER'S TIP

Another important item is the budget for site improvements submitted to the municipality. If this document is available, it should always be included within the report. The municipality will also have site improvement budgets for comparable projects. These can be used by the appraiser to support the site improvement estimate, although developers may structure costs differently.

Inspecting the Neighborhood

The appraiser should get a general feel for the neighborhood because residential support services are very important to the feasibility of a subdivision. For instance, the proximity of schools is extremely important to home buyers. The appraiser should determine if schools are within walking distance or if public or private bus service is available. Proximity to shopping is also very important, especially access to food stores which residents will frequent more than any other type of retail business. The appraiser should note the travel times and convenience of access to necessary services. The distance to regional malls, recreational facilities, and religious institutions should also be considered.

---

2. Douglas D. Lovell and Robert S. Martin, *Subdivision Analysis* (Chicago: Appraisal Institute, 1993), 6.

Inspecting the Site

When the appraiser arrives at the site, he or she should get a general sense of the stage of construction, the topography, and the physical composition of the subdivision. Items to note during the initial site inspection include:

- The clearing and staking out of lots, sanitary sewer grills, detention basins, and utility installation features such as piping protruding from the ground for plumbing.

- Schematics detailing the number and size of lots from a site plan or project brochure. Plans should be acquired before inspecting the site, whenever possible. The appraiser can then compare the layout detailed in the project map with the current state of development and note any positive or negative factors affecting value. Proximity to high-tension power lines, the potential for flooding, proximity to train lines, and other adverse influence are important, and the number of lots affected should be carefully noted. Positive features such as large shade trees, favorable topography, attractive views, and desirable locations for premium lots should also be considered.

- Topography of the site, described in terms of its gradient. Table 6.1 indicates standard classifications for site topography.

Table 6.1—Topography and Grade Classification

GRADE CLASSIFICATION	DESCRIPTION
0% - 2%	Nearly level and/or gently undulating
3% - 8%	Gently sloping and/or undulating
9% - 15%	Moderately sloping and/or rolling
16% - 30%	Strongly sloping and/or hilly
31% - 40%	Steep
Over 40%	Very steep

Source: Appraisal Institute, Subdivision Analysis seminar.

Existing Homes on the Site

Old or new model homes, partially completed units, inventory units, and sold homes may be included in a subdivision appraisal. Usually the appraiser's job is to estimate the value "as is" at a particular moment in time. When a project has gone into receivership, partially completed homes may show signs of neglect and the appraiser must inspect these improvements carefully.

The appraiser should carry a supply of home inspection checklist forms in case some of the units are partially completed. The appraiser can walk through each home and check off which items have been completed or installed to calculate the completion percentage for that unit. Although the appraiser is not a construction inspector, he or she should note any obvious items of functional obsolescence or evidence of poor construction quality. A sample "Subdivision Partial Construction Report" can be found in the appendix to this text.

APARTMENT BUILDINGS

Apartment buildings have some unique features which may complicate their inspection. It is not possible or practical to inspect every unit in a large complex. In appraising most commercial property types, access to individual units is easily arranged. Inspecting an apartment, however, can be an intrusion on someone's living space and arrangements must be made in advance with the property manager or superintendent.

The tenant mix of an apartment project is another important item to be considered. The tenant mix will be partially determined by the number and type of units. A project with a preponderance of efficiency and one-bedroom units will tend to have more transient tenants; a project with many two-bedroom units will have a more stable tenant mix. Vacancy and turnover are often determined by how well the unit mix matches market demand.

Security features and proximity to support services are key issues in valuing apartments, although they may have minimal impact on other property types. The presence of a security guard can improve the marketability and lower the vacancy rate of a project. Building and parking lot lighting are also important. Proximity to support services such as churches, food stores, regional malls, and transportation should be investigated.

Inspection

The following items should be considered in inspecting an apartment building.

- The sample of units inspected should include at least one unit of each type. If units of similar size can have different designs (e.g., several types of two-bedroom units), the appraiser should inspect one of each type and design.

- Although the appraiser will not be able to inspect all the units in a large complex, at least one upper-level unit should be inspected so the appraiser can determine if water leakage is a problem.

- Inspecting the model apartment gives the appraiser an idea of the layout, but not the condition, of a typical unit. Appraisers should always inspect at least one lived-in unit of each type to determine condition and maintenance levels. Obviously, inspecting several units will give the appraiser a better understanding of project construction and condition.

- A wide-angle lens may be needed to photograph the exterior of a large project. Interior photographs of typical units should also be taken.

APPRAISER'S TIP

The appraiser should list the units inspected in the report. If the manager has steered the appraiser away from units with problems, citing the units inspected within the report will provide evidence of this.

- The lighting within the project and on the outside of the buildings should be noted. Good lighting is important for security reasons.

- The number of parking spaces available and the parking ratio are especially important. Sometimes parking spaces are numbered and each tenant is assigned a space. The amount of guest parking available in dedicated lots should also be recorded.

- General project maintenance levels can be determined through observation. Both unit interiors and the building exterior should be evaluated. The quality of the landscaping is a direct reflection of the degree of management, and this is one of the first areas to be neglected when a project becomes insolvent. The appraiser can also ask the tenants how well management is maintaining the project.

- The extent of modernization in an older project is worth noting. Modernization reflects good management and is usually necessary to maintain competitiveness. Typical upgrades include new tile and vanities in bathrooms, new kitchen cabinets, new appliances, additional appliances such as built-in microwave ovens and dishwashers, new air conditioners, and the replacement of old windows with double-pane windows set in aluminum frames. Cosmetic improvements such as fresh paint and new floor coverings are essential.

- Special marketing features should be noted. These may include fireplaces, walk-in closets in the master bedroom, a third bedroom in markets where two bedrooms are the norm, private patios and balconies, and hardwood floors.

- The unit mix is crucial. In many markets, prospective renters must wait for two-bedroom units while one-bedroom and efficiency units comprise virtually all of the project's vacant units.

- The type of heating system can affect the rent charged for apartments. It costs considerably more to heat units with electricity than gas. The appraiser should get into the habit of adjusting the value estimate for this difference when a difference in sale prices is evident in the market.

- The appraiser should visit the building engineer and ask if the project is up to code. If not, it may be necessary to undertake an expensive upgrade program which will significantly affect value. In areas of the country where earthquakes are common, very expensive upgrades may be needed to make a building earthquake-resistant. The local health or fire department can also be contacted regarding safety issues, ADA compliance, and necessary upgrades. High-rise apartment buildings may need sprinklers to meet fire codes.

- Apartment projects of more than three stories will have elevators. It is often not practical for the appraiser to do an elevator inspection because specialized knowledge is required. A disclaimer should be included in the report to limit liability.

- Ideally, apartment units should have separate water heaters and heating units so individual tenants can be billed based on their usage. When a building has common systems, more water and heat are often used by the tenants, and this should be considered in the appraisal.

- The amenities of a project are important to its marketing and long-term vacancy rate. The presence of a pool, tennis courts, jogging paths, playgrounds, and other common areas such as parks and lakes should be noted.

SHOPPING CENTERS

A wide range of items must be considered when inspecting a shopping center. The type of shopping center determines the factors to be evaluated and the weight the appraiser should assign to each. Neighborhood shopping centers without anchor tenants usually have the least tenant-specific design. Community shopping centers with one or more anchor tenants tend to have a more specific tenant mix, which is designed to create synergy between the satellite and anchor tenants. These centers have more specialized characteristics. Regional shopping centers are the most carefully devised and the appraiser must take special note of how well the center's design, layout, and parking serve the needs of the large anchor tenants and satellites.

Site Characteristics

When examining a shopping center site, functional compatibility is of primary importance. The parking lot layout should facilitate traffic ingress and egress. The proximity of parking to the primary building entrances should also be considered. Specific items to be considered may include the angle of parking spaces to facilitate ingress and egress, the direction of traffic flow, the construction of speed bumps to discourage speeding, the funneling of traffic toward the exits, and the adequacy of truck delivery lanes.

The number of parking spaces provided for each 1,000 square feet of gross leasable area provides an indication of how well the site will serve the shopping center's patrons and tenants. Table 6.2 indicates recommended parking areas for shopping centers of various sizes.

Table 6.2—Recommended Parking Parameters				
GROSS LEASABLE AREA (GLA) IN SQUARE FEET	PARKING SPACES PER 1,000 GLA	SQUARE FEET PER SPACE	SQUARE FEET OF PARKING	PER GLA
25,000	4.0	375	37,500	1.50
100,000	4.0	375	150,000	1.50
400,000	4.0	375	600,000	1.50
500,000	4.5	375	843,500	1.690
600,000	5.0	375	1,125,000	1.875

Source: Urban Land Institute, *Parking Requirements for Shopping Centers* (Washington, D.C.: Urban Land Institute, 1982).

The adequacy of parking for disabled shoppers and for store employees should also be determined.

Security and personal safety needs have increased in many areas, so parking lot lighting is particularly important. The appraiser should note how well-illuminated the site is and whether there are any poorly lighted areas. Sometimes decorative lighting can add to the appeal of a center. The presence or absence of security should also be noted, especially in relation to competing centers, which may or may not offer security.

The appraiser should note the availability of excess land for building and parking expansion. The amount of frontage on one or more major streets will directly affect the center's visibility as will the shape of the site and the location of the building on the site. The amount, type, and effectiveness of center and store signage should be noted.

Drainage and topography are especially important for shopping centers. Asphalt paving prevents water drainage and a proper mechanism for channeling water runoff should be in place. Areas of standing water will undoubtedly cause problems if temperatures drop below freezing; as the water freezes, cracks and potholes will form. Most newer centers have detention basins to facilitate water accumulation and runoff.

Inspection of Neighborhood Shopping Centers

The appraiser should look at the following building characteristics during a neighborhood shopping center inspection:

- Exterior design. Concrete block walls along the sides and rear are typical with a combination of concrete block, brick, stucco, wood cedar shake, or metal panels on the facade.

- Exterior facade condition and appeal. Will a facelift be required for the center to be competitive? Does the exterior create a positive image?

- Shape. The shape of the building should contribute to its visibility and facilitate access. The signs placed on the outside should be visible from the street; the shape of the building may increase their visibility. Retail space with limited visibility from street level will usually generate lower rental rates, require more marketing time, and have a higher vacancy rate.

- Canopy. Does the canopy improve or detract from the visibility of the stores and their signs?

- Roof. Typically, neighborhood centers have flat roofs of rubber, asphalt, tar, and gravel or composite shingle gable roofs. Note the presence or absence of a roof guarantee. Guarantees often do not cover problems with flashing or other wear items.

- Windows. Windows are typically large retail glass panes, double-hung on newer centers, with wood or aluminum frames.

- Alarm system. Burglar and fire alarms should be connected to the police department or an independent monitoring service.

- Sprinklers. Sprinklers are usually not found in older centers, but are required for most new construction.

- Building access. Note the presence or absence of handicapped ramps, railings, and wide entrance doors.

- Handicapped restrooms. Larger restrooms may be provided with lower sinks and safety rails. Requirements and codes vary by state.

- Interior lighting. Adequate fluorescent or incandescent lighting should be provided.

- Interior space. The appraiser should note the type of flooring (low-pile carpeting and vinyl tile are standard); type of walls (plaster in older buildings, sheetrock in newer centers); type of wall coverings (wallpaper, paint, paneling); fixed or suspended ceilings with acoustic tile panels; overall physical condition of space; items of noticeable depreciation (commonly worn carpeting and water marks on the ceiling); and type and number of fixtures (including ceiling fans).

- Plumbing system and adequacy.

- Heating system and adequacy.

- Cooling system and adequacy.

- Electrical capacity in each unit. Usually 100- to 400- amp capacity is provided depending on tenant needs; 200 amps is the most common.

- Rear loading access. Tailgate or drive-in loading facilities with sufficient maneuvering area are required.

- Percentage of interior finish and amount of space allocated to office area.

Functional obsolescence. As they age, neighborhood shopping centers usually suffer from less functional obsolescence than community or regional shopping centers. Tenant mix is also less important because tenants are usually not interdependent. Most of the functional obsolescence inherent in neighborhood shopping centers relates to site location and parking considerations. The following list details typical items of functional obsolescence found in neighborhood shopping centers.

- Insufficient employee and/or patron parking. Often employees park along the side or rear of the center.

- A facade that is outdated or does not meet market tastes.

- Insufficient signage on the facade or along the street.

- Building orientation that results in poor visibility, especially in areas of high-speed traffic. Space at the center and rear of the project have the most obsolescence. High vacancy rates and low rents for this space are due to little or no visibility.

- Inadequate electrical capacity.

- Inconvenient access to the center from overcrowded roadways or inconvenient turn lanes.

- Inadequate lighting along the building perimeter and in parking areas.

- Inadequate package heating and cooling systems.

- A location below grade which reduces visibility.

- One or more buildings at the front of the center that obscure its visibility.

- An overhanging canopy that obscures the names of the businesses. Courtyards and recessed units are usually difficult to see from the street.

Inspection of Community Shopping Centers

Community shopping centers share some building characteristics with neighborhood shopping centers, but some additional items must be considered in their inspection. The type of anchor tenant will often determine the center's clientele and therefore the tenants of satellite stores. The appraiser should recognize any apparent synergy within the center and the type of patrons drawn to it. Many centers develop a specialty niche. Because anchor tenants are extremely important to the viability of a community shopping centers, the appraiser should pay particular attention to the design of the anchor store and its functional utility.

Ceiling heights tend to be more variable in community centers. Anchor tenants usually need higher ceilings to accommodate more plumbing lines, electrical fixtures and wiring, and HVAC ducts. Many anchor tenants want a spacious interior, which can be created with higher ceilings. Ceiling heights for anchor tenants usually range from 12 to 18 feet.

A community shopping center site should have sufficient room for the anchor tenants to expand. Many anchor tenants have been lost to the competition because they could not expand their space to meet current demand or to compete with newer, larger rivals.

Loading facilities are important because community centers move a large volume of goods. There should be a sufficient number of loading doors of the proper type and room for trucks to turn. Because community shopping centers have larger trade areas, they are more susceptible to local traffic problems than neighborhood centers. Community shopping centers usually require at least one traffic light to facilitate access. On heavy-volume roadways without a light to lead traffic into the center, access can be inconvenient or unsafe. This has a material effect on the tenants and the profitability of the center.

Inspection of Regional Shopping Centers

The following considerations are significant in describing regional shopping centers.

- Regional shopping centers are often the target of car thieves. As a result, security issues are more pronounced. The appraiser should determine if the lot is monitored by a security staff and cameras and if the lighting is adequate.

- The appraiser should note if the center is enclosed or partially open.

- Space for the delivery of goods must be increased for regional shopping centers. As a general rule, "the delivery space needed to receive merchandise for the various tenants in the shopping center plus service space for dumpsters and miscellaneous refuse should be approximately 10% to 15% of the gross building area."[3]

- Regional centers should be located at the intersection of two major streets with convenient access to an interstate highway.

- The anchors and their signs should be visible from each level of the interior.

- Anchors should have at least one access point on each level of the mall.

- Stores that are competitors should be located on opposite sides of the mall.

- In multilevel malls, common walkways from one side of the center to the other, escalators, and elevators for the handicapped should be easily accessible and convenient.

- Regional malls commonly have at least one food court.

- A theme can give a center additional drawing power.

INDUSTRIAL BUILDINGS

Industrial buildings include warehouses, factories, manufacturing facilities, special-purpose properties, and hybrids containing some combination of office, research and development, manufacturing, and warehousing space. An industrial building located in an area dominated by an industry that is doing poorly can suffer severe external obsolescence. The availability of raw materials, highways, and workers are more important to industrial properties than to other commercial property types. Changes in building design, such as the trend toward higher clear ceiling height or the lack of interest in multistory buildings, can leave an industrial building with a limited market. Increasing taxes and the actions of labor unions can also affect the value and marketability of industrial properties.

Inspection

The following items should be noted during the inspection. The first five relate to the property's linkages—i.e., the time and distance relationships between the property and supporting facilities.

- Proximity to major highways. If trucks must travel through one or more residential areas to get to a highway, the subject may suffer from locational (external) obsolescence compared to properties that are better situated.

- Proximity to public transportation such as a subway, trains, and buses. An isolated location may result in fewer available workers.

- Proximity to airports. If the manufacturing operation requires frequent cargo shipments, proximity to an airport may be crucial. For this reason industrial subdivisions are frequently found near airports.

- Proximity to active freight train lines. Train service can be extremely important to the overall profitability of any business that must bring raw materials to its facility and then ship its products to other locations. High freight rates can result in plant closures if a property is located too far from its markets.

- Proximity to ports and docks.

- Availability of utilities. Industrial buildings require more electricity than most other property types. Plants may require a tremendous amount of water. The availability of

---

3. James D. Vernor and Joseph Rabianski, *Shopping Center Appraisal and Analysis* (Chicago: Appraisal Institute, 1993), 133.

gas is crucial to industries such as glass manufacturing. Certain types of industries require vast sewer capacity to remove the effluent from their manufacturing processes.

- Availability of raw materials. The availability of coal, gas, oil, or minerals and the method by which they are delivered to a manufacturing building can be key to the success or failure of a facility.

- Building frame. Old, multistory industrial buildings with partial or all wood frames are less fire resistant and may suffer from load stress. Newer industrial buildings are typically unaffected.

- Clear ceiling height. As the manufacturing base of the country declines and warehousing increases, higher ceiling heights are demanded. A comparison of newly constructed buildings with those that are 10 or 20 years old reveals this trend very clearly. The difference in clear ceiling heights between manufacturing buildings and warehouses has resulted in two, separate markets in most areas of the country. The appraiser should be aware that higher ceilings can sometimes be an advantage for a manufacturing building, if overhead electrical lines, air lines, and overhead cranes are needed.

- Loading capacity of floors. Most concrete floors in manufacturing buildings are eight inches thick. If the concrete floor is less than six inches thick, many types of heavy machinery cannot be accommodated. Warehouses can have thinner floors, depending on the storage weight of the typical products stored in the building.

- Bay size. The amount of space between steel columns in an industrial building, i.e., the bay size, can significantly affect stacking capacity and the movement of products through the storage area. Too many beams or too little space between them creates functional obsolescence.

- Loading doors and facilities. Heavily developed cities like Chicago and New York have many industrial properties that suffer from insufficient loading facilities. The result is local traffic congestion. An insufficient number and/or type of loading doors can create functional obsolescence depending on market requirements.

- Turning radius. The turning radius, i.e., the amount of space available for tractor trailers to back into a loading door, can have a tremendous effect on property value and marketability. Buildings in heavily developed cities may have very little or no turning radius, which can cause traffic problems.

- Parking. Sufficient parking is needed for employees, delivery vehicles, tractor trailers, and sometimes customers. Many older facilities have insufficient parking compared to modern standards and this can lead to functional obsolescence.

- Elevators. Elevators may be required to transport goods or raw materials between floors.

- Sprinklers. Sprinklers add to the marketability of many types of properties; their absence may create functional obsolescence. Local building codes require sprinklers in many small, newer industrial buildings and they are prevalent in larger buildings and buildings with a higher percentage of office space.

- Police and fire coverage. Industries have different security and police requirements. Manufacturing processes that make use of flammable materials have special fire protection needs.

- Percentage of office space and office composition. Higher percentages of office space are found in research and development facilities and lower percentages in general industrial buildings. Very little office space is included in warehouses.

- Degree of customization for the existing business. If a building has been specially designed for the owner or tenant, it may be a limited-market property. This is usually the case when extensive machinery and equipment have been incorporated into the building to facilitate the manufacturing process.

- Character of the area. Does the area suffer from labor strife or urban problems such as crime and violence? Are there other demographic factors at work in the area that can affect the subject?

- Local labor availability. In addition to a large pool of general manufacturing workers, many industries need specially trained workers who can only come from vocational and technical schools. More middle-level managers may also be needed in the future.

- Taxes and labor union activities. These factors have precipitated the movement of entire industries to less expensive locations, e.g., the textile industry from New England to the South and high-tech companies from California to Utah. Companies may be offered tax reductions for the first five to 10 years or free land as an incentive to move.

- Dependence on an ancillary industry. If an industry goes into decline, those providing ancillary support services or goods may be adversely impacted. For example, automobile parts suppliers were hurt when Detroit had problems in the 1980s. Similarly, the closing of military bases across the country has greatly reduced the need for certain industrial products.

Of course, the basic construction and mechanical components of the building—i.e., lighting, insulation, HVAC system—must be investigated as they would be in any commercial property inspection.

OFFICE BUILDINGS
Office buildings are inherently more complex than other types of commercial properties. Because they are usually multitenanted, more emphasis is placed on the physical factors that affect the marketability of the building. Mechanical components such as plumbing, elevators, sprinkler systems, and HVAC can be extremely complex in multistory office structures.

Classification
Before inspecting an office building, the appraiser considers its classification. A building can be categorized as a trophy building or as Class A, B, or C space. Classification is based on the design, condition, and tenancy of the building.

Trophy buildings usually have a unique design, an uncommon shape, superior locations, and the most desirable tenants. The triangular TransAmerica Tower in San Francisco is one example. Trophy buildings are sometimes identified by their tenant mix. The Empire State Building in New York has both a unique tenant mix and an easily identified shape. Most trophy buildings are extremely well maintained and have responsive, creative management.

Class A buildings have excellent locations, better-than-average tenants, superior construction quality, and the highest rents in their respective markets, second only to trophy buildings. They tend to have very efficient mechanical systems and sometimes offer amenities not found in Class B and C buildings, such as on-site security and restaurants. Class A buildings incorporate electronic features such as "smart" computers to monitor energy usage. They offer tenants superior views and usually have large floor plates. They are classified as investment-grade property.

Class B buildings do not have the high-quality construction of Class A buildings and are often more depreciated. The tenant mix is undistinguished and the space offered has few frills or amenities. Some older Class B buildings were formerly Class A, but changes in design and construction materials made them less attractive. Other older Class B buildings may be historic and have unique construction components, although depreciation will be evident. Their locations can range from average to excellent and their floor plates are usually smaller than those of Class A buildings.

Class C buildings offer few or no additional amenities, are the most depreciated, and have the least desirable locations, usually comparatively far from the city center or important roadways. Management is often of average or below-average quality and the tenants do not have any synergy or prestige. These buildings often have functionally obsolete components such as smaller or outdated elevator systems and older, less efficient HVAC systems. Class C buildings are rarely upgraded to meet newer electrical demands.

Inspection

In inspecting an office building, the appraiser will want to answer the following questions:

- Is the building a multitenanted, single-tenant, government, or medical building (i.e., more than 75% government or medical tenants)?

- Is the building classified as low-rise (one to three stories), mid-rise (four to 15 stories), or high-rise (over 15 stories)?

- What type of frame does the building have? There are many types of framing systems. Wood frames are only found in low-cost, low-rise buildings. For higher buildings, three types of frames are used: steel, reinforced concrete, and composite construction, which is an efficient blend of steel and concrete. Generally, a steel frame is used in low- and mid-rise buildings, a reinforced concrete frame is seen in more expensive low-rise buildings such as research and development facilities, and composite construction is prevalent in high-rises. Although the frame may not be visible, the building plans usually describe the type of frame used.

- Does the building have "smart" features and design? Smart components include fiber optic cabling; special wiring for computers and videoconferencing; electrical, heating, and cooling systems that are computer-controlled for maximum efficiency; and air filtration devices. Some buildings have special mechanical systems which reduce noise or emissions.

- Have the lighting ballasts been upgraded to meet the standards set forth in the Energy Policy Act of 1992? To reduce mercury concentrations in the atmosphere, 8-ft., 4-ft., and 2-ft. U-shaped fluorescent bulbs are no longer being produced. The newer bulbs produce less heat and save up to a third of electricity costs.

- Is the building sprinklered? Are there any sprinkler violations that must be cured prior to the sale of the building?

- What type of safety systems and design features are present in the building? Safety systems may include highly responsive smoke and fire alarm systems, sprinkler systems, and specific emergency stairwell exits. Many office buildings have standpipes, fire hoses, portable fire extinguishers, and specialized heat and smoke detection systems.

- Is asbestos present and, if so, is it friable? Has the asbestos been encapsulated so that it cannot become friable and spread through the building?

- What is the gross building area, the net rentable area, and the usable area? The only practical way to determine usable area, commonly known as *lockup area*, is to examine building floor plans.

- What is the building's efficiency ratio—i.e., the ratio of rentable area to total gross building area? In general, the efficiency ratio should be 85% or greater. If the subject has a lower efficiency ratio than comparable buildings of the same class, an adjustment for functional obsolescence may be required.

- Is sufficient parking available? Inadequate parking can be a significant form of functional obsolescence. The parking requirements at the time of the building's construction may have been lower than today's standards. Some urban buildings have no parking area, which is often an item of functional obsolescence that significantly impacts value and marketing time. Buildings with below- or above-ground parking included in the building design may have a marketing edge over those with no parking.

- Has the building been upgraded to conform to the Americans with Disabilities Act? Standard ADA disclaimers should be included in the assumptions and limiting conditions section and in other parts in the report if necessary.

- Are any special services or amenities offered—e.g., restaurants, round-the-clock security, day care, gymnasiums, parking decks?

- What types of maintenance contracts are in place? Typical contracts include elevator maintenance agreements, heating system agreements, air-conditioning system contracts, security arrangements, outside management agreements, and cleaning contracts.

- Do any other features enhance the appeal of the building? Office buildings may have security cameras monitoring all open areas, specialized mail conveyance systems, or strategically placed elevators that offer views of the outside or a central foyer.

- Is the fire protection system adequate? An office building should have at least two fire exit stairs in case one becomes blocked. Some older buildings in urban areas have metal fire escapes attached to the outside of the structure. Although this is allowable, it is not desirable. If the subject is to be modernized, these exterior fire escapes will likely be replaced with interior fire exits, which will greatly increase the cost of modernization.

- Is the building's design optimal? The column spacing in an office building can cause marketability and value problems, which are often overlooked in commercial appraisals. If the columns are too close, the offices constructed around them will be too small. Many large users of office space want extensive open areas that can be divided into cubicles to house many employees. Insufficient column spacing may interfere with an efficient layout, limiting the market for the space. Older buildings are often subject to this type of functional obsolescence, which must be considered within the appraisal.

- Are the windows properly placed? Some older buildings have windows which are set too high up on the walls or are too small to provide desirable views. This can reduce the marketability of the space and affect value. A functional obsolescence adjustment may be necessary if the market perceives this to be a detriment. The cost to cure this type of obsolescence can be substantial.

SUMMARY

A great many items must be considered in commercial property inspections. Condition and construction materials must be noted in all commercial property inspections, while items such as clear ceiling height and elevators are significant only to certain property types. Functional obsolescence is more prevalent in commercial properties because they are subject to a wider range of variables than residential properties. To conduct a thorough inspection, the appraiser must become knowledgeable about a wide range of property-specific items. Experience and inspection skill usually takes years to develop and there is always more to learn.

APPENDIX

Subdivision Partial Construction Report

Property Observation Checklist

Types of Houses

Subdivision Partial Construction Report

Lot number	Inspection date
Project	Block/lot

Site		% of Job	Interior		% of Job
Sidewalks & curbs	○	1.0%	Rough plumbing	○	3.5%
Paving	○	1.0%	Rough heating	○	2.0%
Grading & seeding	○	0.5%	Stairs	○	2.0%
			Rough electric	○	1.5%
			Insulation	○	1.0%
Exterior		**% of Job**	Sheetrock	○	4.0%
Water line/well	○	1.0%	Spackling	○	1.0%
Sewer line/septic	○	1.0%	Subflooring	○	1.0%
Excavation	○	6.0%	Interior door set	○	1.0%
Footings	○	2.5%	Trim	○	3.5%
Foundation walls	○	9.0%	Vinyl flooring	○	0.5%
Concrete floor slabs	○	2.5%	Ceramic tile baths	○	0.5%
Framing, walls	○	18.5%	Plumbing fixtures	○	0.5%
Framing, roof	○	2.5%	Finished plumbing	○	2.0%
Sheathing	○	4.0%	Finished electric	○	1.0%
Roofing	○	2.5%	Finished HVAC	○	1.5%
Garage door set	○	0.5%	Light fixtures	○	0.5%
Patio doors	○	1.0%	Built-in equipment	○	1.5%
Porches/platforms	○	0.5%	Hardware	○	0.5%
Gutters & leaders	○	0.5%	Hardwood/carpet	○	0.5%
Exterior painting	○	1.0%			

APPRAISAL
INSTITUTE®

PROPERTY OBSERVATION CHECKLIST

LIMITED SCOPE ANALYSIS

The Property Observation Checklist is a limited scope analysis voluntarily prepared by the appraiser during the normal course of his/her inspection of the subject property in the preparation of a real estate appraisal. In completing the checklist, only visual observations are recorded. The intent of the checklist is to identify possible environmental factors that could be observable by a non-environmental professional. The appraiser did not search title, interview the current or prior owners, or do any research beyond that normally associated with the appraisal process, unless otherwise stated.

The user of this checklist is reminded that all responses to the questions are provided by an appraiser who is not an environmental professional and is not specifically trained or qualified to identify potential environmental problems; therefore, it should be used only to assist the appraiser's client in determining whether an environmental professional is required. The checklist was not developed for use with single-family residential or agricultural properties.

The appraiser is not liable for the lack of detection or identification of possible environmental factors. The appraisal report and/or the Property Observation Checklist must not be considered under any circumstances to be an environmental site assessment of the property as would be performed by an environmental professional.

GENERAL INSTRUCTIONS

The appraiser should distinguish, as appropriate, between the physical presence of possible environmental factors and the economic effect such factors may have in the marketplace or on the value estimate. In completing the checklist, the appraiser should attach reports, photographs, interview records, notes, public records, etc., as documentation for specific observations. The instructions for each section of the checklist specify the kinds of documentation required.

If, for any reason, this checklist is prepared as a stand-alone document, it must be accompanied by an attached statement of limiting conditions and certification of the appraiser's qualifications.

TERMINOLOGY AND APPRAISAL STANDARDS

The following checklist terms appear in *The Dictionary of Real Estate Appraisal,* third edition (Chicago: Appraisal Institute, 1993) and are specifically referenced in the Property Observation Checklist: *adjoining properties; environmental professional; environmental site assessment;* and *pits, ponds, or lagoons.* Please refer to *The Dictionary of Real Estate Appraisal,* third edition, for discussions of these terms.

Please refer to Guide Note 8, "The Consideration of Hazardous Substances in the Appraisal Process," *Guide Notes to the Standards of Professional Appraisal Practice* (Chicago, Appraisal Institute, 1995); Advisory Opinion G-9, "Responsibility of Appraisers Concerning Toxic or Hazardous Substances Contamination," *Uniform Standards of Professional Appraisal Practice* (Washington, D.C.: The Appraisal Foundation, 1995 ed.); and other appropriate statements in the professional standards documents for additional information.

Describe the appraiser's on-site inspection of the subject property and, as applicable, the adjoining properties:

_____

_____

_____

_____

SECTION 2   Possible Environmental Factors Observed by the Appraiser

Indicate below if any of the following possible environmental factors were observed during the appraiser's visual inspection(s) of the subject property and, as applicable, the adjoining properties. A written description of possible environmental factors should be provided for all questions where "Yes" is checked.

1. Did the appraiser observe an indication of current or past industrial/manufacturing use on the subject property or adjoining properties?

   ○ Yes   ○ No   **If observed, describe below:**

_____

_____

2. Did the appraiser observe any containers, storage drums, or disposal devices not labeled or identified as to contents or use on the subject property?

   ○ Yes   ○ No   **If observed, describe below:**

_____

_____

3. Did the appraiser observe any stained soil or distressed vegetation on the subject property?

   ○ Yes   ○ No   **If observed, describe below:**

_____

_____

4. Did the appraiser observe any pits, ponds, or lagoons on the subject property?

   ○ Yes   ○ No   **If observed, describe below:**

_____

_____

5. Did the appraiser observe any evidence of above-ground or underground storage tanks (e.g., tanks, vent pipes, etc.) on the subject property?

   ○ Yes   ○ No   **If observed, describe below:**

_____

_____

6. Did the appraiser observe any flooring, drains, or walls associated with the subject property that are stained or that emit unusual odors?

   ○ Yes   ○ No   **If observed, describe below:**

   _____

   _____

7. Did the appraiser observe any water being discharged on or from the subject property?

   ○ Yes   ○ No   **If observed, describe below:**

   _____

   _____

8. Did the appraiser observe any indication of dumping, burying, or burning on the subject property?

   ○ Yes   ○ No   **If observed, describe below:**

   _____

   _____

9. Did the appraiser observe any chipped, blistered, or peeled paint on the subject property?

   ○ Yes   ○ No   **If observed, describe below:**

   _____

   _____

10. Did the appraiser observe any sprayed-on insulation, pipe wrapping, duct wrapping, etc., on the subject property?

    ○ Yes   ○ No   **If observed, describe below:**

    _____

    _____

11. Did the appraiser observe any transmission towers (electrical, microwave, etc.) on the subject property or adjoining properties?

    ○ Yes   ○ No   **If observed, describe below:**

    _____

    _____

12. Did the appraiser observe any coastal areas, rivers, streams, springs, lakes, swamps, marshes, or water-courses on the subject property or adjoining properties?

    ○ Yes   ○ No   **If observed, describe below:**

    _____

    _____

13. Did the appraiser observe any other factors that might indicate the need for investigation(s) by an environmental professional?

    ○ Yes   ○ No   **If observed, describe below:**

    _____

    _____

3 of 4

Indicate below if in completing this assignment the appraiser was informed—verbally or in writing—of any information concerning possible environmental factors reported by others. "Others" may include the client, the property owner, the property owner's agent, or any other person conveying such information. Documentation should be provided for all instances where "Yes" is checked. If the information was presented verbally, then a written description of the source and circumstance of the communication should be attached to this checklist and/or the appraisal report. Copies of printed reports provided to the appraiser should be attached to this checklist and/or the appraisal report.

14. Has the appraiser been informed about federal- or state-maintained records indicating that environmentally sensitive sites are located on the subject property or adjoining properties?

    ○ Yes   ○ No   **If yes, provide documentation.**

15. Has the appraiser been informed about past or current violations (e.g., liens, government notifications, etc.) of environmental laws concerning the subject property?

    ○ Yes   ○ No   **If yes, provide documentation.**

16. Has the appraiser been informed about past or current environmental lawsuits or administrative proceedings concerning the subject property?

    ○ Yes   ○ No   **If yes, provide documentation.**

17. Has the appraiser been informed about past or current tests for lead-based paint or other lead hazards on the subject property?

    ○ Yes   ○ No   **If yes, provide documentation.**

18. Has the appraiser been informed about past or current tests for asbestos-containing materials on the subject property?

    ○ Yes   ○ No   **If yes, provide documentation.**

19. Has the appraiser been informed about past or current tests for radon on the subject property?

    ○ Yes   ○ No   **If yes, provide documentation.**

20. Has the appraiser been informed about past or current tests for soil or groundwater contamination on the subject property?

    ○ Yes   ○ No   **If yes, provide documentation.**

21. Has the appraiser been informed about other professional environmental site assessment(s) of the subject property?

    ○ Yes   ○ No   **If yes, provide documentation.**

_____

Signature

_____

Name

_____

Date Checklist Signed

_____

State Certification or   State State License #

4 of 4

TYPES OF HOUSES

There are five basic types of single-family houses: single-story, two-story, one and one-half story, bi-level, and split level. Other types of housing include townhouses and condominiums. Housing types are often perceived differently by home buyers and the appraiser must be aware of the advantages and disadvantages of each type.

SINGLE-STORY HOME

The most common architectural style for a one-story home is the ranch. In a one-story home, all the living area is on the ground floor, although a basement or crawl space may be present. Single-story homes tend to be relatively simple in design and they enjoy wide market acceptance. Many home buyers prefer a home without stairs. The layout of a single-story home is depicted in Figure 1.

Single-story homes have the following advantages:

- Easily constructed.
- Relatively easy to maintain.
- Can have several entrances and exits.
- Absence of stairs may appeal to the elderly or handicapped.
- Found in almost all markets and accepted by home buyers.
- Relatively easy to expand.

Figure 1—Single-Story House

Courtesy of Henry S. Harrison, *Houses—The Illustrated Guide to Construction, Design & Systems,* 2d ed. (Chicago: Residential Sales Council of the Realtors National Marketing Institute, 1992).

The disadvantages of single-story homes include:

- More land is often required and home expansion may be constrained on smaller lots.
- With all the rooms located on one floor, noise and traffic can spread throughout the house.
- May be more expensive to build due to the high ratio of foundation and roof area to living area.
- Some home buyers perceive single-story homes on slabs to be colder in the winter since all the living area is located near ground level.

- Where land values are high, one-story homes may be perceived as tract developments, senior citizen housing, or homes for the less affluent.

TWO-STORY HOME

A two-story home is usually designed with the living areas (dining room, living room, kitchen, den, etc.) on the ground floor and the bedrooms and bathrooms on the second floor. Most architectural styles are reflected in two-story homes.

The advantages of a two-story home include:

- Separation of living areas and bedrooms.
- Allows for greater intensity of development on small lots. In areas with high land values, this may be the only type of home that will be profitable for a developer to build.
- Less land is required for building.
- Foundation and roof costs are less than for single-story homes.
- Some home buyers perceive two-story homes on a slab to be warmer in the winter than single-story homes because the second floor is not exposed to the cold ground.
- The most expensive homes are almost always two-story.

Figure 2—Two-Story House

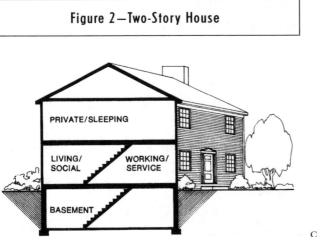

Courtesy of Henry S. Harrison

The disadvantages of a two-story house are:

- Some home buyers perceive stairs to be a negative feature.
- The second floor is rarely accessible from exterior stairs, increasing fire risk.
- Expansion is usually limited to the first floor.

ONE AND ONE-HALF STORY HOME

This type of home usually has the living area and at least one bedroom and bath on the ground floor with other bedrooms and a bath on the second floor. The architectural style of one and one-half story homes is usually Cape Cod, although other styles can be associated with it.

The advantages of a one and one-half story home include:

- Relatively compact and less expensive to heat.

- The second floor may be unfinished, giving the owner the option of finishing it later; a lower purchaser price can usually be negotiated when the second floor is unfinished.

- Has the appeal of both one-story and two-story homes.

Figure 3—One and One-Half Story House

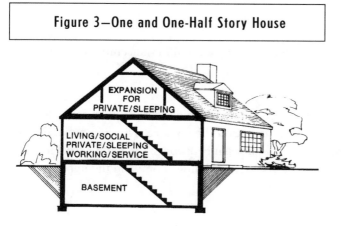

Courtesy of Henry S. Harrison

The disadvantages of these homes are:

- Traffic through the home must use the stairs.

- The market may consider this type of house to be outdated.

- Furniture may be difficult to move upstairs.

BI-LEVEL HOME
A bi-level home is characterized by a first-floor level that is four feet or less below ground level and a second level that is completely above ground. The first floor usually contains a recreation room, family room, or bedroom. The second floor contains the living area of the home. The architectural style most often associated with bi-levels is the raised ranch or split-foyer home. A bi-level home is depicted in Figure 4.

The advantages of a bi-level home include:

- Expansion can be easily accommodated.

- The lower level is usually regarded as gross living area, not basement space.

Figure 4—Bi-level House

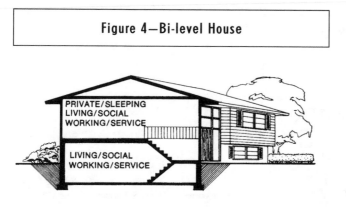

Courtesy of Henry S. Harrison

- When unfinished, such homes are usually affordable. Unfinished bi-levels can be finished later at the owner's discretion.

The disadvantages of a bi-level are:

- The lower level is usually perceived as cold and damp unless it has a superior heating system and insulation.

- Ducts are difficult to install.

- Interior traffic must use the stairs, which are usually located in the central portion of the home.

SPLIT-LEVEL HOME

A split-level is a hybrid consisting of a bi-level section and a single-story section. If the house has a basement, it may be called a tri-level or a quad-level. Living area is found on two floors. The lower level may contain a garage, den, and additional bedrooms; the middle level includes the kitchen, foyer, laundry room, living room, and dining room; and the upper level contains the bedrooms and bathrooms.

The advantages of a split-level home include:

- Efficient traffic flow throughout the house.

- An unfinished lower section can be finished at the owner's discretion and often results in a lower purchase price.

- Split-levels are easily adapted to rolling terrain and lots with irregular topography.

- The lower level is usually considered part of the gross living area.

- Expansion can be accommodated.

- Furniture can be relocated with ease because the levels are separated by only a few steps.

- The various zones of the home are divided and noise is reduced.

The disadvantages of a split-level home are:

- Relatively limited architectural styles.

- If the topography is flat, some markets perceive this type of home to be less attractive.

- The heating and cooling may be irregular due to the separation of zones within the home.

- Some markets perceive this style of home to be functionally obsolete. As a result, developers rarely build new split-levels.

Figure 5—Split-level House

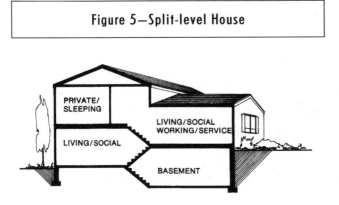

Courtesy of Henry S. Harrison

TOWNHOUSES

Often referred to as row houses, duplexes, triplexes, or even fourplexes, townhouses are single-family homes that share at least one common wall with an adjacent home. As land values increase, townhouses become more prevalent because they allow for a much higher density of development. In highly urbanized areas, they may be the only type of housing that can be profitably built on small, expensive lots. In some areas, townhouse development is the most efficient development plan. Many municipalities require developers of townhouses to set aside a significant amount of land for open space.

The benefits of townhouses include:

- Higher density of development, often resulting in more profit.
- When little land is available, this may be one of the few profitable development alternatives.
- A garage for the home owner.
- Lower site improvement expenses due to cluster development.
- Appealing to home owners who do not wish to landscape or maintain a property.
- Amenities such as tennis courts and pools are often available.
- Project landscaping, snow removal, exterior and roof repairs, and upgrading may be provided without the assistance of the home owner.

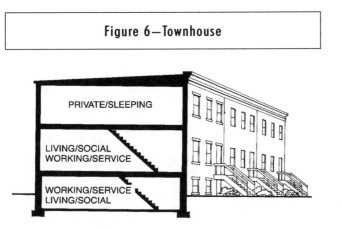

Figure 6—Townhouse

PRIVATE/SLEEPING

LIVING/SOCIAL
WORKING/SERVICE

WORKING/SERVICE
LIVING/SOCIAL

Courtesy of Henry S. Harrison

The disadvantages of townhouses include:

- Common walls may carry noise from neighboring homes.
- There are limits on the amount of space available for planting.
- Restrictive covenants present limitations—e.g., no air-conditioning units in the windows, no miniature satellite dishes, no outside antennae.
- Problems with one or more units may require repairs for the entire development. For example, the entire roof may need to be replaced when only a few residents are having problems.
- Many townhouse projects do not have basements although some have a loft or third floor. This can present storage problems.

CONDOMINIUMS

Free-standing condominiums are similar to townhouses in most respects. However, they rarely have garages; resident and guest parking lots usually fill this need. Condominium owners have more common walls with their neighbors. Condominiums generally fall into four categories: units in resort areas where high land values necessitate multifamily housing, entry-level and first-time home buyer projects, affordable housing, and senior housing. Most of the advantages and disadvantages of a townhouse apply to condominiums.

BIBLIOGRAPHY

BOOKS AND SEMINARS

Appraisal Institute. *Appraising Residential Properties.* 2d ed. Chicago: Appraisal Institute, 1994.

Appraisal Institute. Appraisal Review—Income Properties seminar. Chicago: Appraisal Institute, 1993.

Appraisal Institute. Dynamics of Office Building Valuation seminar. Chicago: Appraisal Institute, April 1995.

Appraisal Institute. Residential Property Construction & Inspection seminar. Chicago: Appraisal Institute, 1994.

Appraisal Institute. Subdivision Analysis seminar. Chicago: Appraisal Institute, 1993.

Lovell, Douglas D. and Robert S. Martin. *Subdivision Analysis.* Chicago: Appraisal Institute, 1993.

National Association of Women in Construction, Greater Phoenix Arizona Chapter #98. *Construction Dictionary.* 8th ed. Phoenix: National Association of Women in Construction, 1991.

O'Connell, Daniel J. *The Appraisal of Apartment Buildings.* New York: John Wiley & Sons, 1989.

Vernor, James D. and Joseph Rabianski. *Shopping Center Appraisal and Analysis.* Chicago: Appraisal Institute, 1993.

White, John Robert. *The Office Building: From Concept to Investment Reality.* Chicago: Appraisal Institute, American Society of Real Estate Counselors, and the Society of Industrial and Office Realtors, 1993.

REPORTS AND PAMPHLETS

The following reports and pamphlets are available from the American Society of Home Inspectors in Arlington, Virginia:

"All About Roofs" (1989)
"Electrical Power and Safety in Your Home" (1989)
"The Facts About Exterior Walls" (1989)
"Give Your Attic a Breath of Fresh Air" (1989).
"Wet Basements and Crawl Spaces" (1989)
"Your Plumbing System" (1991)

ARTICLES

De Vries, Dwayne and Alexander Meisel. "Assessment for Disabled Access Surveys: New Opportunities for Home Inspectors." *The ASHI Reporter* (September 1995): 14-15.

Peck, Jerry. "Voltage Detectors." *The ASHI Reporter* (May 1995): 24.

Wiley, Robert. "Liability Insurance Corner." *Appraiser Gram* (December 1994): 3.